Writers of Wales

Editors
MEIC STEPHENS   R. BRINLEY JONES

D0912694

William R. Lewis

JOHN GWILYM JONES

University of Wales Press

Cardiff 1994

With the exception of Saunders Lewis, few modern Welsh twentieth-century writers have commanded as much veneration in their own lifetime as did John Gwilym Jones. In 1973, two years after retiring from his readership in the Department of Welsh at the University College of North Wales, Bangor, he was awarded an honorary D.Lit. by the University of Wales, and in the year before his death in 1988 he was elected Fellow of the Welsh Academy. He acknowledged these accolades with childlike delight and gratitude, but close friends could detect in him a certain degree of bewilderment. This was understandable in view of his somewhat fortuitous and unanticipated rise to academic prominence at a time when literary study in Wales was considered to be the prestigious domain of literary historians, textual critics and philologists.

On 27 December 1904, John William Jones – later to be known as John Gwilym Jones – was born at Y Groeslon, a small village a few miles to the south of Caernarfon. He was the only son of Griffith and Jane Jones, both of whom were of local stock: his father's family from Clynnog and his mother's from Llandwrog. Griffith was a stonemason and even at an early age had a mind of his own. When he was twelve, both he and his brother received a harsh beating from their headmaster and as a result they both left school for good. As John Gwilym Jones recalls in his autobiography AR DRAWS AC AR HYD (*Here and There*), the most potent influence on Griffith's subsequent education would be the chapel and the eisteddfod: *We had at home a Commentary on every book in the Bible . . . My father used to compose very polished compositions for local eisteddfodau and had immense pleasure in doing so.* However, he was not a dominant father-figure: *My father was a quiet man, and to be quite honest, when I was a child, I hardly knew him.* More often than not, Griffith worked away from home and he would shower his son with gifts in an attempt to compensate for his frequent absences. Although he attended chapel regularly, Griffith loathed the religious orthodoxy of his upbringing and towards the end of his life, fascinated by the new liberal theology of the age, he became something of an agnostic. Before his death at the age of eighty-four he suffered a severe stroke which dramatically transformed his personality. John Gwilym Jones describes his father's last years with some bitterness:

Constantly I had to tell him off and sit him in his chair. He would laugh at me. It was strange for me to see him changed so much: things which had probably been suppressed came to the fore when there was no longer anything to restrain them.

His portrayal of Griffith in the autobiography is affectionately respectful but lacking in detail. We are left in no doubt that the dominant figure in his life was Jane, his mother.

Jane Jones was a strong-willed, domineering and intelligent woman. Her childhood at Llandwrog had been harsh. Two of her brothers died of diphtheria in childhood and her father was to die of pneumonia when she was only twelve, leaving her mother to bring up Jane, Maggie and one brother, John. During Jane's childhood the 'Tithe War' was at its height, and her father had been amongst those who protested against the requirement that a tenant had to pay a tithe to the Anglican incumbent regardless of that tenant's religious affiliation. The autobiography mentions one particular incident that involved John Gwilym Jones's grandfather:

All the houses [at Llandwrog] were owned by the large Glynllifon Estate and my grandfather was the only man in the village who did not work for the estate. It was the time of the Tithe War and some of the people of Y Groeslon decided to show their opposition by making an effigy of Mr Jones the Parson, carrying it in a coffin down to Llandwrog and burning it in front of the Ty'n Llan tavern. A message came from Glynllifon that nobody from Llandwrog was to go near the place and that they were to stay in their houses and close the curtains. My grandfather did go . . . and the next morning a notice came instructing him to leave his house.

Jane was to inherit her father's radicalism, and John Gwilym Jones proudly recalls the fact that she and Griffith – no doubt at her prompting – were amongst the 609 individuals who voted for Lewis Valentine in Plaid Cymru's first election campaign.

Jane had spent a number of years in service in Liverpool and so, unlike the monoglot Griffith, she could speak English, and she was widely read. She was also deeply religious, a committed Calvinistic Methodist who accepted unquestioningly the fundamental tenets of her denomination. The *seiat*, the prayer meeting and the literary meetings at Brynrhos Chapel were the mainstay of her life and she insisted, much to her son's irritation, that he should regard them likewise. But she too, before her death, appeared to have lost her early enthusiasm for religion.

Although John Gwilym Jones in later life rejected the existence of God, one does not encounter in his creative works that vitriolic loathing of Welsh Nonconformity found in Anglo-Welsh writers such as Caradoc Evans. In fact he never rejected the basic principles of Christian morality. When he returned to live at Y Groeslon he attended Brynrhos Chapel regularly, and as evidenced in CAPEL AC YSGOL (*Chapel and School*), the Pen-y-groes Library Annual Lecture which he delivered in 1970, he looked back upon certain aspects of his religious upbringing with gratitude:

> . . . *it gave me a respect for words as a measured outpouring of high quality, lithe, majestic Welsh which penetrated, without my knowing it, the depths of my being. It gave me a grounding of biblical and theological knowledge without which I could not have responded to Christian poets such as Pantycelyn and Euros Bowen and Gwenallt Jones whose use of biblical allusion is such a living thing, nor indeed to unbelieving dramatists such as Samuel Beckett.*

At home Jane was a stern disciplinarian and such was the strength of her personality that her son grew up *a frightened and nervous child*. It has often been asserted that the domineering mother figure who often appears in his works is based upon Jane. One should not take this too literally, even though he concedes in his autobiography that many of his characters and situations are based on individuals and incidents in his own childhood. The creative process, by its very nature, is complex. Characters, although often based upon a writer's impressions of real people, function only within the framework of the artist's imaginative vision.

In childhood, John Gwilym Jones appears to have suffered from being constantly ridiculed by his friends for his cowardice. He was always the muffish outsider observing with a mixture of frustration and relish the misdemeanours of his peers. The only refuge to which he could escape from emotional trauma was Cae Doctor, his grandmother's home at Llandwrog a few miles down the road from Y Groeslon.

Being at Llandwrog was *like stepping into another world*. At that time Y Groeslon was a flourishing quarrying village whereas Llandwrog was predominantly rural and agricultural in character. His recollections of these visits are vivid and affectionate:

There was plenty to do at Cae Doctor. I loved playing on the riverbank or in the river, and an odd river it was in that it changed its name from field to field. The feat was to catch fish with my hands beneath the stones, and to venture under the bridge near the house was quite an adventure for a small child.

At times his work shows a tendency to idealize and romanticize rural life and this may possibly be related to his warm recollections of visits to Llandwrog. It is significant that his more emotionally stable characters such as Ianto and Sir William in Y BRODYR (*The Brothers*), Nesta, despite her cruel upbringing, in Y DEWIS (*The Choice*), and even Alis in AC ETO NID MYFI (*And Yet Not I*) are products of a changeless, unsophisticated and often amoral rural community whereas his emotionally complex characters tend to come from a more educated, competitive, self-conscious and puritanical quarrying community which was more open to intellectual and social change.

From 1908 until 1916 he was a pupil at Penfforddfelen Primary School where the curriculum was traditional, the discipline harsh, and the language of instruction English. The years at Penfforddfelen were important in two respects. Firstly, he was much influenced by one of the teachers, W. O. Jones, who ensured that his young protégés in the scholarship class had a thorough grasp of grammar and in particular of clause analysis. Throughout his teaching career, even at university level, John Gwilym Jones was a staunch traditionalist, and his students at Bangor were constantly reminded that a mastery of grammar and syntax was essential for aspiring writers. Secondly, it was at Penfforddfelen that he forged what was to be a close lifelong friendship with Thomas Parry, who, in an illustrious academic career, became Professor of Welsh at Bangor, the National Librarian of Wales and subsequently the Principal of the University College of Wales at Aberystwyth.

Much to the delight of his ambitious mother, John Gwilym Jones passed the scholarship examination and, in 1916, gained a place at Pen-y-groes Grammar School. Two of the teachers there were to have a profound influence upon him: Mr David Davies his English teacher and Miss Priscilla Kate Owen his Welsh teacher. David Davies had the ability to mesmerize his class: *I remember his reading Macbeth and, to this day, I can recite almost all of Macbeth from memory from beginning to end because he made such an impression upon me.* And it was Miss Owen who not only instilled in him an awareness of the locality's rich cultural heritage but also encouraged his literary talents. CARIAD PLENTYN (*A Child's Love*), an early attempt at play-writing, has survived from this period in manuscript form, and remains in the family's possession.

Having passed the Higher School Certificate and after a year as a pupil-teacher at his old primary school, he and his friend Thomas Parry entered the University College of North Wales, Bangor in 1922. It was during registration at Bangor that he was advised by Sir Ifor Williams, the Professor of Welsh, to change his name from John William Jones to avoid confusion with another student of the same name. Thus, John 'Gwilym' Jones registered as a first-year student to read Welsh, English, Latin and philosophy.

At Pen-y-groes he had decided to sit his Higher examinations after one year in the sixth form rather than two. This may have had a bearing on his somewhat disappointing results which meant that he had to study for an Ordinary Degree in Welsh and economics rather than a Single Honours Degree in Welsh. This was a bitter blow from which, even in later life, he never fully recovered. Indeed, it could be argued that the overt intellectualism of his characters has its roots in the author's own academic inferiority complex. It is as if he wanted to show his true intellectual capabilities and wide cultural interests through these characters.

Unlike Thomas Parry, who served on various student committees, he remained something of an outsider while at college. There is a scene in AC ETO NID MYFI in which the principal character, Huw, is deeply offended by not having been invited to join an informal literary circle. This scene is founded on fact: it appears that John Gwilym Jones was not considered worthy to be numbered amongst the illustrious ranks of Bangor's literary élite. However, he was actively involved in the Choral Society and the Welsh Dramatic Society.

As a schoolboy he had seen and enjoyed local amateur companies performing the plays of W. J. Gruffydd, D. J. Davies and R. E. Jones (Gwynfor) at Y Groeslon, but he had not yet experienced the thrill of professional theatre. It was a visit to the Empire Theatre, Liverpool with Thomas Parry *that first awakened [in him] a real interest in drama.* Sybil Thorndike was playing the role of St Joan. It was an experience which he never forgot: *I can see Sybil Thorndike now on the stage in the darkness and a kind of holy light upon her and I can hear her saying, 'How long, O Lord? How long?'*

His involvement in the activities of the Welsh Dramatic Society at Bangor was to prove equally inspiring. The mainstay of the Welsh Dramatic Society was J. J. Williams, headmaster of Cefnfaes Secondary School, Bethesda. In Welsh dramatic circles he was regarded as one of the most accomplished directors of his day. His production of Ibsen's A DOLL'S HOUSE was considered at the time to be an important milestone in the development of modern Welsh theatre. More than anything else John Gwilym Jones admired his emphasis on voice and expression:

He would show an actor how to open his mouth and that it was the lips that should form the words. I do not find that Welsh actors do that. Those of the North especially tend to speak gutturally instead of hitting the consonant as should be done in Welsh. To me Welsh is something jagged not something smooth

. . . To him good articulation was absolutely essential and enunciation had to be absolutely clear in every play he produced.

Yet, despite the fact that he became secretary and treasurer of the Society and attended all its rehearsals, only once was he offered an acting part. He was one of the elderly farmers in a production of J. O. Francis's play GWYNTOEDD CROESION (*Cross Currents*).

After graduating in 1925 in Welsh and economics he followed a one-year teachers' training course and, in 1926, having applied unsuccessfully for numerous teaching posts, he was at last accepted by the education authority in London and put on its 'List of First Appointments'. For a while he taught in a city school and then at Hoxton where the poverty shocked him, before moving on to Millfields Road Elementary School in Hackney.

The period in London was crucial to his development as a playwright and director in that it reinforced what had been instilled in him by J. J. Williams at Bangor: that drama is an artistic form that calls for mastery of language not only on the part of the playwright but equally on the part of the performer. What he most admired about such actresses as Edith Evans and Gwen Ffrangcon Davies whom he saw regularly at The Old Vic was, to quote from an interview, *their respect for the written text and their articulation of the English language.* As a literary critic and adjudicator he could be forgiving in the extreme, but as a director he could be scathing in his criticism of actors, especially professional Welsh actors who wrongly emphasized a word or phrase or whose pronunciation displayed affectation.

In 1930 at his parents' request he successfully applied for an English post at Llandudno Central School. His first few months back in Wales were unhappy ones: he longed for the hustle and bustle of London Welsh life, in particular the social activities centred on the Welsh Calvinistic Methodist Chapel in Charing Cross Road. However, his longing for London was eased within a year when two of his London friends, O. M. Roberts and William Vaughan Jones, also came to teach in Llandudno and the three of them became actively involved in the Welsh cultural life of that town. John Gwilym Jones not only directed numerous school productions but also productions for the Llandudno Dramatic Society.

It was whilst he was at Llandudno that his mother died from cancer. Despite her influence on his early years he was philosophical about her death:

Mother died in 1937 and, although it is a terrible thing to say, I was glad that she was allowed to die. She was in so much pain that she craved for anything that could alleviate it . . . I was glad to see her released from her suffering.

But it was Jane's death which prompted him to start writing in earnest. In 1939 he gained national recognition when he won both the Drama Medal and the Literature Medal at the National Eisteddfod at Denbigh; the former for a full-length play entitled DIOFAL YW DIM (*He Who's Down Need Fear No Fall*) and the latter for a short novel entitled Y DEWIS.

In 1944 he moved to Pwllheli Grammar School to teach English and a little Arithmetic to junior classes. Eventually he was allowed to prepare pupils for the Senior Certificate in English, a task which he found challenging in a rural Welsh-speaking area. On one occasion he was asked by the headmaster, R. E. Hughes, to prepare pupils for the Senior Certificate in scripture. The headmaster was concerned that many of his pupils failed the subject because of their lack of English. John Gwilym Jones, who, of course, was not a believer, recalls this intellectual challenge with amusing irony: *twelve of them gained what was called a Distinction. Indeed, five of them entered the ministry and I can after all congratulate myself for making a substantial contribution to religion!*

Again at Pwllheli he became an enthusiastic member of the town's dramatic society. The playwright Huw Roberts recalls a rehearsal of a translation of J. B. Priestley's TIME AND THE CONWAYS:

The rehearsals were a revelation to me. John Gwilym had little interest in technical matters, such as sets and lighting, which he preferred to leave to others; but his reading of the text and his handling of actors had a very sure touch. He was very good at what might be called stage mechanics and the devising of stage business that illuminated the text and, more important to me, he would often explain his reasoning.

I remember clearly, realizing during this period what could be done by the relative placing of actors on stage, by effective entrance and exit, by gesture, timing and periods of silence. I suppose the word to use about him is 'inspirational'.

During the war John Gwilym Jones was a conscientious objector but his autobiography tends to play down his pacifism:

Because I was a teacher and of a certain age I had no difficulty in refusing to appear before a tribunal or anything of that kind but I did choose to do voluntary work at the hospital when I was in Llandudno. I was not by nature a politically inclined person and I did not attend any pacifist meetings.

This position appears to be consistent with his artistic vision. In his works he is no propagandist. Indeed, he is deeply suspicious of any form of idealism. Ifan's pacifism in DIOFAL YW DIM ultimately wrecks his life; in LLE MYNNO'R GWYNT (*Where the Wind Listeth*) Dewi's desire to join the war in order to enrich his artistic vision is treated sympathetically, whilst Janet's loathing of Huw's pacifism in the same play is prompted by sheer bitterness and hatred.

However, according to his lifelong friend O. M. Roberts with whom he taught at Llandudno, John Gwilym Jones's pacifism was motivated by his uncompromising nationalism. He made no secret of his opposition to the English 'warmongering' establishment. In an interview with the author, O. M. Roberts maintained that:

. . . *he hated Churchill and all he stood for. Often he would barge into the staff room with a newspaper in his hand and, regardless of those present who supported the war, would voice his disapproval of Churchill's conduct of the war. To avoid embarrassing confrontations I often had to tell him to keep quiet.*

How should one interpret these contradictions? It may well be the case that in later life he regretted having embraced such an extremist position towards what, in retrospect, was arguably a just war. This is doubtful. A more likely explanation is that he would not allow his personal convictions to overrule his deterministic artistic vision. As a determinist, he believed that our actions are predetermined and that free will and individual choice are no more than an illusion. Thus, he could not but shy away from moral judgement. Writers who embrace this pessimistic philosophy are inclined to focus upon emotional crises in family life rather than upon political and social crises which for the individual inevitably involve moral choices in the face of injustice and evil. Ibsen's most overtly deterministic works such as HEDDA GABLER and GHOSTS are also his most claustrophobic. Determinism of the hard kind is arguably the most apolitical of all philosophies. As we shall see, in John Gwilym Jones's last play, YR ADDUNED (*The Vow*), Ifan's political convictions, however worthy, do not inspire him to write his play.

He left Pwllheli in 1947 and taught for a year at his old school at Pen-y-groes. Alwyn Roberts, one of his former pupils and now a Vice-Principal of the University College of North Wales, Bangor, maintains that John Gwilym Jones's concern with grammar and correctness was indicative of something more fundamental:

In retrospect and with a greater understanding of John Gwilym Jones, I am sure that he was saying rather important things about himself in this concern about the teaching of a language. Perhaps there are three elements to this: it was an expression of a writer's respect for language, of a craftsman's respect for the tools of his craft and, although this is as hypothetical as some of his own literary interpretations, it was a means of expressing something about the way he saw the world . . . grammar has to do with a language's development and tradition, development over centuries of use as a means of communication.

In 1948 he joined the BBC at Bangor as a producer of radio talks but within a short while became a drama producer. These were pioneering times and playwrights who understood the demands of radio were scarce. Competent actors were in short supply: more often than not experienced actors were already employed. The late W. II. Roberts in his auto-biography admired John Gwilym Jones's concern for detail: *[He taught me] to appreciate the timing of a word and the rhythm of a sentence.* Likewise, the late Charles Williams acknowledged in his autobiography that being directed by him was like being at college.

Whilst still working for the BBC he had been invited by the Welsh Dramatic Society of the University College at Bangor to direct its productions, but his appointment as a lecturer in the Department of Welsh in 1953 was unexpected. Principal Sir Emrys Evans had been impressed by a talk which he had given in English to the Bangor Rotary Club on the subject 'Words'. A week later a letter arrived from Sir Emrys inviting him to an interview during which, much to his astonishment, he was offered a lectureship in the college's Department of Welsh.

The appointment was controversial in some Welsh circles as it was felt that he lacked the necessary academic credentials for the post. However, John Gwilym Jones would prove that these fears were unfounded, and he was revered by his students as a lecturer of outstanding ability. At the time the department did not offer a formal course in creative writing: more often than not students were stimulated to write because he instilled in them a profound love of literature. The poets Gwyn Thomas, Derec Llwyd Morgan, Alan Llwyd, Nesta Wyn Jones and Einir Jones gratefully acknowledge his influence upon them; likewise novelists such as Eigra Lewis Roberts and John Rowlands.

But to many students his name will always be

synonymous with the Welsh Dramatic Society. He directed more than thirty productions for the Society, as well as finding time to direct numerous productions for other drama societies in his own locality. Most of his major plays were written specifically for the Society and directed by him. On the whole the actors were inexperienced and so his directorial style at times tended to be benignly autocratic. The emphasis was on correct enunciation of dialogue and meaningful, disciplined gesture rather than upon self-expression and self-exploration. Not all the students became professional actors, broadcasters, or directors but those who did, like John Ogwen, Maureen Rhys, Dafydd Huw Williams, Norman Williams, R. Alun Evans, Cenwyn Edwards, Alun Ffred, Ifan Roberts, William Jones, Elwyn Jones and John Pierce Jones, have all made a significant contribution to Welsh theatre, television and radio.

John Gwilym Jones also became one of Wales's most influential literary critics. The main thrust of his criticism is to be found in two volumes published in 1977: SWYDDOGAETH BEIRNIADAETH (*The Function of Criticism*), a collection of lectures, articles and eisteddfod adjudications compiled by Sir Thomas Parry, and CREFFT Y LLENOR (*The Writer's Craft*). His other published works are on specific authors and include WILLIAM WILLIAMS PANTYCELYN (1969), a bilingual study of the eighteenth-century Welsh Methodist hymn writer, and DANIEL OWEN – ASTUDIAETH (1970) a study of the nineteenth-century Welsh novelist, based on his MA thesis. There are also two published lectures: in 1976, NOFELYDD YR WYDDGRUG (*The Mold Novelist*) about Daniel Owen, and in 1981 YR ARWR YN Y THEATR (*The Hero in the Theatre*). His lecture on the eighteenth-century poet

Goronwy Owen, delivered at William and Mary College Virginia in 1969, was also published under the title GORONWY OWEN'S VIRGINIAN ADVENTURE.

This book will confine itself to John Gwilym Jones's creative work, but it is worth noting that, although as a critic and lecturer he dealt with writers from a variety of periods and traditions, he would, if pressed, admit to his preference for those who mirrored his own personal vision of life. A great writer or poet, he would argue, always succeeds in capturing with *compassion* life's inherent ambivalences and paradoxes, giving *expression to man's life . . . in its entirety.* Great works for him are those that are *soul-stirringly conscious of life's vigorous energy and also agonizingly conscious of its deadly brutality.*

Inevitably the personal views of some writers, dramatists and poets prevent them from achieving this ideal. For example, he finds W. J. Gruffydd's early poetry too subjective to be deemed great poetry; Daniel Owen's Calvinism produces a lack of compassion towards some of his characters, and consequently excludes him from the ranks of great novelists; the absurdist vision of life expressed by Beckett and Ionesco is as one-sided and *sentimental* as the most maudlin of lyric poetry. Likewise satire as a genre, since *its function is to criticize sharply without [displaying] a trace of compassion.* However, he found a kindred spirit in the poet R. Williams Parry, whose poetry is a *mixture of sadness and joy, of confidence and despair, of love and hate* and therefore appeals to *every inclination and taste.*

In his emphasis on the *close reading* of texts one can

detect, to a large degree, the influence of the 'Practical Criticism' of the Cambridge critic I. A. Richards. John Gwilym Jones, like Richards, appreciated the equilibrium and synthesis of conflicting emotions in a great poem; and like F. R. Leavis, another English critic whom he admired, he believed that a poem should engage both the mind and the feelings of its reader. However, he did not embrace their antagonism towards modern culture nor did he regard literature as a substitute for religion which is, to quote Richards, *capable of saving us* and is *a perfectly possible means of overcoming chaos*. Unlike Leavis, who was preoccupied with the *essential Englishness* of certain poets and writers and their standing in relation to a tradition, John Gwilym Jones, despite his nationalist convictions, was not concerned with the 'essential Welshness' of a particular writer. In his view great literature, because it deals with the fundamentals of human nature, transcends national boundaries and cultures.

～

John Gwilym Jones's work does not fall clearly into distinguishable periods because his vision of life remained remarkably unchanged throughout his literary career. As a non-believer he did not consider human existence to be a God-given gift. For him an individual's life is not governed by external moral precepts but by personality, which in turn is governed by impersonal forces beyond the control of the individual, such as heredity and environment.

Yet, some individuals, again by virtue of their personality, find it easier than others to come to terms with the paradoxes and ambivalences of life.

They acquire for themselves some form of individual freedom, however imperfect it may appear. Some may even be able to rationalize these paradoxes and ambivalences into an ideal, a religious or an artistic vision, but again it is their intrinsic make-up that enables them to do so. Others – indeed the majority of his characters – overwhelmed by the forces of heredity and environment, are unable to realize their aspirations. Life is an agonizing struggle with their own personalities. Idealism occasions despair; parental ambition occasions tragedy; the desire for individual freedom occasions public ridicule and most poignantly of all, particularly so in his later plays, sexuality causes personal anguish and self-revulsion.

His first work to be published was a play called Y BRODYR, probably in 1934, although no date is shown in the published work. Gwennan Tomos, in her MA thesis on the work of John Gwilym Jones, suggests that this play may have been one of the unsuccessful entries for the full-length play competition at the National Eisteddfod at Wrexham in 1933. He did win the prize for a short play at the same eisteddfod but unfortunately that play was never published.

In Y BRODYR the action alternates between 'The Other Side' and the real world. As copies of the play are scarce a detailed synopsis of the plot may be helpful.

Ianto, a footman, has recently died and is greeted affectionately on 'the other side' by his former master, Sir William, a genial aristocrat who had died ten years previously. Ianto is wearing a red ribbon across his shoulders, a symbol of the burdens of the world. Sir

William, who died a contented man, is able to remove this ribbon, thus enabling Ianto to enter eternal bliss.

Mali, a young girl who is already on 'The Other Side', is not so fortunate. She, too, is wearing a red ribbon and is eagerly waiting for her lover, Alun, to arrive so that he can remove it. When Alun appears he is unable to fulfil this task because he has not died a contented man. Alun was a doctor who, having witnessed the cruel death of his father from cancer, had devoted his whole life to finding a cure for the disease. He has died leaving the work unfinished. Until he experiences recognition for his work and in its wake, personal fame, he will not be in a position to enable himself or Mali to experience eternal bliss.

To resolve their predicament Mali and Alun decide to help Idris, Alun's younger brother, to proceed with the research. Because they are in this wretched state of limbo, Mali and Alun cannot appeal to people's better nature, only to their inherent selfishness. However, they hope that if Idris succeeds in his research, he has enough common decency to declare the truth, thus releasing Alun from his torments.

Idris, against his will but encouraged by the ambitions of his domineering mother Jane, is about to leave for London to study medicine. He is a creative individual who wants to be a poet and whose aspirations are encouraged by his sister Gwen. When Jane reminds him of his father's suffering, Idris, who like his father before him, is a weak individual, succumbs and much to Gwen's chagrin accepts from his mother a box containing Alun's research papers.

When Idris begins to read these papers he hears Alun's voice from 'The Other Side'. He promises not to steal Alun's ideas and decides to burn the papers, but Alun, in an appeal to Idris's baser instincts, tells him not to do so: Idris should take advantage of this unique opportunity to become famous.

Eight years have passed and the world is about to hear of Idris's research work. Alun has experienced joy in helping Idris, but the creative Idris has throughout these years been distracted by the attractions of London's artistic life. Paradoxically, Alun hopes that it is this creative element within him that will enable him to proclaim the truth.

The final scene takes place outside a conference hall where Idris's research is about to be announced to the world. Dr Price Evans, an eminent physician, greets the proud mother. He explains that Idris's research is far superior to Alun's and that the findings have helped his own patients. A reporter arrives but, as Price Evans and Jane are about to be photographed, Idris appears with his sister Gwen. Idris rebukes his mother for seeking publicity, and the reporter, accompanied by Price Evans and Jane, goes elsewhere to be photographed. Gwen and Idris admit to their hatred of their mother and her selfish ambitions. Idris guiltily tells Gwen about the papers and the voice encouraging him to proceed with the research. Gwen attempts to persuade him to reveal all but Idris cannot face the impending personal predicament. There is only one course of action for him: suicide. He pulls out a gun, runs to an adjoining room and shoots himself. A hysterical Gwen interprets this as just revenge for their mother's warped desires. The reporter returns and opens the door of the adjoining room and somewhat nonchalantly remarks: 'Heavens above! What a story!'

Despite its well-crafted scenic progression the play has a fundamental weakness: the playwright has touched upon too many themes within the framework of one play. At a superficial level it is a play about the unreasonable educational ambitions of Welsh parents for their children in the years following the First World War. At a more profound level it can be interpreted as a play about a domineering mother's destructive influence upon her children, especially the more creative of the two, Idris, who lacks the courage to realize his deepest desires. Since Idris has inherited this weakness from his father, another recurring theme in the play is heredity. Alun and Jane Owen, too, seem to have strikingly similar personalities and aspirations.

It is regrettable that Sir William and Ianto are abandoned as soon as they have played their role in the narrative, for it is these two somewhat amoral individuals who stand for normality in the play: neither of them has any great mission in life; they accept, to quote Sir William, *the inevitable*. Unlike Alun and Idris they die contentedly. Another weakness stems from the tendency for decisions taken by the main characters to result from off-stage reflection rather than stage action and to be expressed in rather florid and protracted speeches:

ALUN: Mali . . . you know something . . . which I don't.
MALI: Yes, Alun . . . Yes. I struggled so hard against it. I despised it . . . I mocked it.
ALUN: You must tell me.
MALI: But it came . . . like a river overflowing its banks. It swept me off my feet. I was utterly helpless . . . but so happy . . . so marvellously painless . . . light as a leaf . . . and prepared to be hurled anywhere. I experienced every virtue and every beauty. Every white flower became a thousand times whiter . . . and its fragrance like nard . . . and there was music there, Alun . . . and tenderness . . . and laughter. It's calling me . . . constantly calling me. I can't withstand it. At first I tried . . . but I gradually realized that . . . that I didn't want to withstand it. I only longed for more and more of it.

The reader is left with the feeling that the dramatist is searching for an appropriate language for a newly-educated, anguished and insecure inter-war generation but has not found one. However, this first play is significant because its many themes prefigure those of his later, more accomplished works.

In DIOFAL YW DIM, the play which won the Drama Medal at Denbigh in 1939, we again encounter a widowed mother, Grace Hughes – in this case not as domineering as Jane in Y BRODYR – who has two gifted sons. The younger, Ifan, is a teacher of Welsh at the local county school whilst Edwin is a sanatorium patient suffering from terminal tuberculosis. It is at this sanatorium that the action begins. Once again, since copies are not plentiful, a summary of the play follows.

Edwin is finding it difficult to come to terms with his illness. However, he is told by a fellow patient that before long he will be able to accept his fate because his illness will bring a perverse nihilistic joy into his life.

At home, Ifan, a failed writer and pacifist explains to his girlfriend and colleague, Beth, that he yearns for a meaningful mission in life. By contrast all that Beth desires is a *simple unassuming life*. His grandfather Thomas, a retired minister, is oblivious to Ifan's predicament. In a senile world of his own he serenely recites from memory extracts from hymns and prose classics. Ifan's pacifism is given a fresh impetus when his mother, Grace, informs him that his late father, on his final visit from the front, had declared that he abhorred the war. She also tells Ifan that he was conceived after this traumatic admission. After hearing this, Ifan decides that from now on he will be his *father's missionary*.

Meanwhile, Dic, one of Ifan's ablest pupils and his most ardent admirer, has become infatuated with Beth. Whilst rehearsing a school play he makes somewhat clumsy advances to her but is overcome by self-revulsion. It becomes apparent that Dic's feelings towards Ifan are ambivalent: he both admires him and loathes him. He too, like Beth, yearns for a simple ordinary existence.

By now Ifan's headmaster is concerned that Dic, influenced by Ifan's pacifism, has rejected a job offer at Durtford Arsenal. Dic is warned that if this became known Ifan would lose his teaching post. Ifan is about to address a peace rally at Caernarfon. Dic, out of sheer jealousy, has threatened to betray Ifan, and Beth tries to persuade Ifan not to go, but to no avail.

In a Caernarfon pub the landlord and one of his regulars Mili, a prostitute, are able to watch through the window as events unfold at the meeting. The other regular, Wmffra, an alcoholic, is too inebriated to respond coherently to the ensuing situation. When the meeting turns into a fracas the landlord opens his doors to provide Ifan and Beth with a safe refuge. They enter the pub with Dic, pursued by a raucous mob. In trying to protect Ifan from the mob, Beth is accidentally struck. Ashamed of what has happened the mob leaves. Ifan, dishevelled and uncommunicative is led out by Beth. Throughout the commotion Beth has ignored Dic and he swears to revenge himself by betraying Ifan.

After his betrayal by Dic, Ifan loses his teaching post and is devastated. Dic should have been *the embodiment of everything he [wished] Wales to be.* (Ifan is not aware of Dic's true motive for revenge and Beth swears to Grace that he will never be told.) Nothing now awaits Ifan save *a dark void . . . disappointment, despair, heartbreak and darkness.* Grace cynically suggests that such a fate always awaits any individual who tries *to do something great in the world.*

Ifan's despair is exacerbated when he hears of Dic's suicide. The play ends with Ifan, already a consumptive, joining Edwin in the sanatorium. Edwin advises him, as he himself was advised at the beginning of the play, *to live [his] own little life.* His *disease will bring [him] happiness.* Ifan will in due course accept this *sick philosophy* of life.

DIOFAL YW DIM should not be interpreted simply as a play about the futility and destructiveness of idealism when it takes precedence over human feelings. The playwright attempts to answer a more fundamental question: what motivates the idealist? Implicit in the play is the notion that 'ideals' do not exist as objective principles. There only exist 'idealists', whose aspirations, however worthy, are governed by forces beyond their personal control:

IFAN: . . . *I don't preach these things deliberately but instinctively . . . I cannot stop doing so because I am what I am.*

Ifan's idealism is a trait which he has inherited from his dead father but, paradoxically, as the first scene with Edwin in the sanatorium implies, this family is also prone to feelings of disillusionment and despair.

Dic is also at the mercy of inexplicable compulsions. On an intellectual level he reveres Ifan but out of jealousy he betrays him:

DIC: . . . *I constantly do things without my knowing.*

Both characters, independently of each other, are conscious of their predicaments and their inability to come to terms with their existence. Dic opts for suicide: Ifan will opt for a slower death. But neither is censured directly or indirectly by the playwright. Indeed his delineation of both characters is sympathetic and compassionate. Their fate is inevitable, predetermined.

24

Although one can detect a certain degree of sympathy towards Grace who finds comfort in reliving the past and wants Beth to do the same, this approach to life is not offered as an alternative to unfettered idealism. Grace, and no doubt her name has a symbolic significance, is fortunate in that she has inherited her stoicism from her father. Nor should one interpret old Thomas's habit of reciting hymns as a sign of his inner tranquillity. Instead it can be compared with Wmffra's drunken maundering about the immortality of the soul in the pub scene. It matters little in the end that one is a retired minister and the other an alcoholic. Both characters have rejected the world and are as moribund as the terminally ill patients in the sanatorium.

In its attempts to grapple with contemporary affairs – nationalism, pacifism and the burning of the Penyberth Bombing School – the play has a vitality that is perhaps lacking in Y BRODYR. Technically, too, it is a better play. Its principal themes are more clearly established and its characters better de-lineated. Theatrically, the most powerful scene is the pub scene which verbally and visually captures the quintessential theme of the play: the absurdity not only of idealism but also of human existence.

The novel Y DEWIS, published in 1942 deals with the personal crisis facing a young boy, Caleb, who has promised his domineering mother that he will enter the ministry. This vow is taken under intimidating circumstances – beside his father's grave the evening after the funeral:

'Caleb' and there was yearning in her voice, 'you know what your father's most passionate wish was.'

'I know,' he said quietly.

'It's your wish as well isn't it?'

'Mother . . .'

'Isn't it Caleb?'

'Yes.'

'I want you to fulfil his wish, Caleb.' She spoke now like someone sure of herself. A host of things rushed into Caleb's mind – many an achievement from the past, a myriad of ideals for the future. He tried to speak but was silenced by his mother. 'You must,' she said calmly, 'dedicate your whole life to the service of God. Many will tell you that there are many ways of doing that. Probably there are but your father knew of only one true way.'

By now Caleb was listening like someone bewitched by her gentle low voice to which passion had added a magical trembling. He lost his will; he felt utterly powerless and he submitted himself to his mother, soul and body.

One could too easily assume that Caleb when he meditates upon the majesty and mystery of the heavens is an orthodox believer:

Whose command did the sun and the moon, the planets and stars obey? She had only one answer to these questions – God, the father of Jesus Christ, who also sent the Holy Spirit into the world, the Holy Trinity and the Three in One. He felt certain that he was behind them all, sitting on his throne of pure gold, robed in glory and beauty . . . There around him were the saints of the ages proclaiming with loud voice – 'Hosanna, Alleluia, The Holy One, The Holy One.' . . . There in their midst was one who was very dear to Caleb.

Such an assumption would be mistaken. In a convincing argument in the CYFROL DEYRNGED, Derec Llwyd Morgan has proposed that Caleb's cosmology is 'pre-Newtonian' and that the religion which Caleb professes has degenerated into what Professor Morgan describes as *superstitious sentimentalism*. Caleb's *Te Deum* is no more than a child's yearning for cosmic order in the face of personal loss. It is not an affirmation of faith but a contradictory and confused cosmology. Caleb's father is not only *amongst the saints* but also in the graveyard watching them:

Your father can see us . . . he is looking at us this minute, with his two large black eyes . . . you do believe that don't you, Caleb?'
  'Yes, mother.'

The remainder of the novel relates Caleb's traumatic endeavour to come to terms with his vow to enter the ministry. Despite being on amicable terms with his school friends he is something of an outsider, admired for his intellect. Words are his forte and like Alun in Y BRODYR and Ifan in DIOFAL YW DIM he too has ambitions to become a writer. He dotes on Shakespeare, especially MACBETH, in which he perceives disturbing parallels between the *vaulting ambition* of Lady Macbeth and that of his mother:

Macbeth's misfortune was the misfortune of the man who kept his promise. Had he broken it his story would have been very different . . . What if he, Caleb, at some time felt like breaking his promise? There was little danger of his doing so, of course, but what would happen if he were to feel like that at some time?

His mother is anxious that he should succeed in his matriculation examination, and his fear of disappointing her becomes an obsession. His sole comfort is visiting his grandmother's house where he can escape into a world of local fable and romance.

When his grandmother dies unexpectedly, Caleb makes another vow: *he would give his grandmother immortality so that she might live for ever in the literature of his country.*

Caleb falls in love with Nesta, a young girl whose mother had died at her birth. She has suffered in childhood because Nansi, her eldest sister, holds her responsible for their mother's death. Their father, Morris Lloyd, feels the same, but, unlike Nansi, is able to suppress his loathing of Nesta.

Like Caleb, Nesta is a creative soul: a promising artist. She encourages Caleb to make a third vow, this time to her. He will inform his mother of his real aspirations and declare publicly at a chapel meeting that he cannot enter the ministry. However, when the time arrives, he cannot fulfil his promise to Nesta. Whilst one of the elders is praying, Caleb comes to a decision. If he were to enter the ministry he would be at liberty to employ his verbal talents:

No longer was there a world nor an existence, no longer mother nor father nor grandmother nor Nesta. Only he himself and words . . . They swaggered in front of him in the full glory of their raiment sometimes ready to dazzle with the brilliance of the two-edged sword of their eloquence . . .

By taking this seemingly cowardly decision Caleb has succumbed to his instincts rather than to his intellect. It is a compromise, but his ebullience after the chapel meeting – *Words! Words! Words! A feast of words! A hurly-burly of words. Intoxicating words flowing like Seithennin's ale* – suggests that, as far as his personal contentment is concerned, he has taken the right decision.

28

Nesta's artistic vision is more sophisticated. Ironically, it is kindled by Caleb's inability to keep his vow to his mother. Her feelings towards him become ambivalent and she *experiences the purity of longing as well as the cutting-edge of doubt.* The compulsion to grapple with these contradictions may in the future prove artistically rewarding, and at the end of the novel she ponders the sight of a tumbledown cottage:

Nesta stood and looked at it. And suddenly, in the moonlight, its ugliness was transformed into beauty . . . For the first time in her life she saw the magnificence of something ugly.

This all-encompassing vision occasions within her a passion for life and creativity. Like the Virgin Mary she feels blessed amongst women for she too is a bearer of new life, and the novel ends with Nesta reciting the 'Magnificat'.

It is doubtful whether Caleb will share her rejoicing. Their estrangement is inevitable. The novelist does not deliberate at length upon his fate. However, if one accepts Derec Llwyd Morgan's assertion that Caleb is a product of a decaying religious culture one should not expect his fate to be anything but ambiguous.

Compared with Y BRODYR and DIOFAL YW DIM, Y DEWIS is a more mature and less pessimistic work. In the plays, both Alun and Ifan are unable to accept life's cruelties and paradoxes and they opt for death. But in this novel Caleb, despite his cowardice and sensitivity, is able to come to some kind of compromise with life, however ill-defined that compromise may be. All is not lost. But it is Nesta who is the embodiment of hope, for she is able to confront life's paradoxes and employ them as a source of artistic vision.

Some of these paradoxes and ironies inherent in human life are depicted in agonizing detail in a collection of short stories published in 1946 under the title Y GOEDEN EIRIN (*The Plum Tree*). The irony of the story 'Y Briodas' (*The Wedding*) lies in the fact that on this apparently joyous and unifying occasion, all the characters, despite putting on a façade of normality, in fact retreat into their own private worlds of unfulfilled hopes, fears and fantasies. The dominant theme is alienation.

The old minister who conducts the ceremony feels that after a lifetime in the ministry he is by now *deep in the furrow* of routine and convention – *like Pavlov's dogs racing instinctively, subconsciously to a certain sound , at certain times.* Yet when invited by the bridegroom to conduct the ceremony he delights in the fact that his *life has not been completely in vain.*

The father also reflects upon his own humdrum existence:

'Catrin, where's my stud?' 'How do I know? Where did you put it?' 'If Lizzie Mary were here, she'd find her father's stud in no time.' . . . 'The rice pudding is not as good as usual.' 'Isn't it?' 'Far too runny.'

The bridegroom is preoccupied with his own literary aspirations. However, he loves his bride despite her unsophisticated tastes:

Lizzie, often, I readily admit, has the intellect for English penny

books and the bold print of newspapers and Hollywood films.
She has no clue about politics and literature and Reaction and
Revolt in the former like the latter mean nothing to her. But she
is my lover and that's what's important.

Lizzie, the bride, is disenchanted with her own
wedding. She had dreamed that her marriage would
have been a forced marriage akin to the one in the
Welsh nineteenth-century romance, THE MAID OF
CEFN YDFA:

But at last after many tribulations, after suffering a mother and
father's cruelty, after writing in blood from my own arm, I was
forced to stand painfully at Maddocks's side in the church like
a languishing lily . . . and outside somewhere was Wil. Don't
break you heart, Wil. Before long the Maid of Cefn Ydfa will be
lying quietly in the churchyard and Wales will be singing your
pastoral song . . .

Or perhaps she would marry a film star: *By my side*
stood a fine figure of a man, a man amongst men, like
Clark Gable in He Adored Her.

Marrying above her station had had its fascination:

'I'm taking a fortnight's holiday this year,' my father told the
steward, 'to stay with my daughter in Bumford Hall.' 'I'm
going to Paris' said Gwen, my sister. 'To Paris?' 'Yes, with
Lady Elizabeth.' 'Lady Elizabeth?' 'My sister, Lady Elizabeth
Bumford, you know.'

But she had resigned herself to her fate. She is
marrying someone like myself and knows that she *is*
doing the right and sensible thing.

Robin, the best man, fantasizes about Lizzie. He
regards himself as *someone who covets his neighbour's*

wife and experiences overwhelming guilt. But he can contain these feelings by experiencing *a kind of mystical uplift, some kind of purification* which enables him to look upon his self-revulsion dispassionately and objectively. He is impelled to this ecstatic state by *poetry, a good sermon, a Bach fugue, clear reasoning, paintings, acting, a high mass . . .* By distancing himself from Lizzie during the ceremony he can *feel her nearness without having wanton thoughts.*

The bridesmaid, Gwen, is even more of a romantic than her sister Lizzie:

I am the Holy Grail. I am the blessed vessel kept by Joseph of Arimathea. Here I am in Pelles' court, the grandfather of Galahad, in the full glory of my holiness, pure, a virgin, like Mary, undefiled, immaculate.

Arthur, the chapel's minister and the best man's elder brother, has not been invited to conduct the ceremony. This fact only confirms his instinctive suspicion that his existence is that of a second-rater: *I always took second place.* He yearns for *mystical insight like Saint John of the Cross, Saint Theresa and Ann Griffiths* but, infatuated by the bridesmaid's *full lips and young breasts,* he cannot reconcile his spirituality with his lustfulness.

But there are deeper ironies in this story. After the old minister's cynical musings, Robin's reference to his *honest tone* is indeed poignant. Arthur, the tormented young minister, yearns for mystical detachment but it is his brother Robin who experiences such detachment apparently without great personal effort. It is ironic too that Arthur is the imagined knight in Gwen's dreams, but he will never know that.

The title-story 'Y Goeden Eirin', probably inspired by Alexander Reid's short story 'Two Tales of Conscience', concerns the fate of a set of twins, Wil and Sionyn. From their conception they were inseparable:

We were conceived at exactly the same time, in the same place and by the same person . . . for years I did not know that we were different. Wil was Wil and Sionyn was Wil.

However, one day, Sionyn, the narrator, falls from a plum tree in their garden and has to stay at home for weeks. For the first time in his life he begins to ponder the nature of the God who planted the plum tree. At first, he appears to be a benevolent being: *I'm very willing to enjoy his good things . . . God is responsible for the sun and moon and the stars and the sea and all that is within it . . .*

Sionyn accepts that this God has given individuals the ability to choose between good and evil. One can choose to be a tyrannical Nebuchadnezzar or a pious Daniel. But he soon discovers that such a notion is simplistic. Even Nebuchadnezzar had his virtues: *he made Babylon the most beautiful city in the world at that time*; and Daniel his shortcomings: *(Daniel) didn't lose five minutes' sleep trying to alleviate the suffering of his fellow slaves on the banks of the Euphrates.* He also becomes increasingly aware of life's paradoxes and perplexities. Wil had joined the war, not out of conviction – ironically Wil is the kinder of the two – but out of an obsessional fear of death. As a child, Wil had seen a young boy in his coffin; going to war was, paradoxically, a way of escaping from this morbid fear. Despite being a pacifist, Sionyn's attitude towards the war is ambivalent.

'Isn't it a pity that Wil hasn't made a stand like Sionyn,' said Mr Williams, the minister. 'We're very fortunate to have people like Wil,' I said to him, 'or we would be trampled under foot.'

After the accident, the twins are no longer inseparable: *today, Wil, my brother, is in Egypt and I am working on the land at Maes Mawr.*

Derec Llwyd Morgan, in the CYFROL DEYRNGED, interprets this story in traditional Christian theological terms. He contends that the plum tree is the 'Tree of Life' itself and Sionyn's fall symbolizes man's 'fall from grace'. In my opinion, the god portrayed by Sionyn is not the traditional, orthodox, Christian God who will perhaps one day bring the twins together again: there is no suggestion that either grace or salvation is at hand. This god is an impersonal absurd force which, for no apparent logical reason, planted the plum tree in an absurd spot in the garden – *between the privy and the wall* – from which, again for no apparent logical reason, Sionyn accidentally falls and, as a result, loses his innocence and experiences the trauma of alienation.

In 'Y Garnedd Uchaf' (*The Highest Cairn*) a condemned prisoner is visited by a minister. The prisoner, once a respected pillar of the community, has led a double-life for years. Of his own volition he has confessed to the murder of his lover Lili Saunders. The minister, unheard by the prisoner, regards this visit as a unique opportunity at long last to give a meaning to his calling: *Here is an opportunity for me to affirm my faith, to be given certainty of your mercy; an opportunity for me to justify long years of working in your vineyard.*

But when the minister mentions repentance the prisoner brazenly professes his atheism:

'I don't believe in God . . .'
 'But my boy . . .'
 'I've never ever repented anything.'

In his imagination the prisoner recalls his past. He is proud of his deeds:

He never felt ashamed about any one of his deeds, be it a lie, a deception, a robbery, a killing. To him they were a pattern of slick dishonesty, of skilful sins, of sure, conscious steps to destruction . . . feats one could pride oneself in.

Even from early childhood the prisoner could look upon his misdeeds coldly and objectively. Having physically forced a fellow pupil to remove his trousers, he saw him *as something dead in his imagination.* He regards his life of crime as a perverse spiritual quest, akin to a climb up a cairn: *And so, on and on from step to step, from step to step. Up? Down? To me, up to the grey pinnacles, groping from their mist to the light of safety . . .*

Gassing his pregnant lover was the high point of the quest. The murder had a *poetic beauty.* At the crest of the cairn in its *wondrous light* he arrogantly asks himself: *Is there anything more that I should do?* And when he blasphemously pours scorn on fundamental Christian tenets even the minister has doubts about his own faith: *Are you the Lamb of God which takest away the sins of the world? What am I? A bundle of passions? The effects of environment and past generations?*

The prisoner feigns repentance and, to the relief and joy of the minister, pleads for God's mercy. But the minister had been no more than a *tool in an experiment – the greatest experiment of his life, a fitting end before oblivion.*

In his book in the *Llên y Llenor* series, John Rowlands argues that the minister is as wretched an individual as the prisoner. But one could go a step further and suggest that ironically it is the prisoner, despite his perverse philosophy of life, who has discovered his true self. The minister's ecstasy, *his song of praise to his Lord*, is founded on a lie and he returns to his study a pathetic, deluded figure.

In 'Y Cymun' (*Communion*) Meurig Lewis, a minister, has met Gwyn, an aspiring young composer, while walking in the mountains. They reach a valley, Dyffryn Ysig. Although Gwyn is familiar with the surrounding landscape – his parents had taken him there on numerous occasions – he feels no deep attachment to the place. Indeed, he is scornful of such concepts as tradition, inheritance and succession: *the only inheritance worth having is the one you gain yourself.* This inheritance is gained by means of the intellect *through sweat and labour.*

Meurig, the illegitimate child brought up in an orphanage, yearns to be at one with the landscape: it would be his ideal inheritance. Unexpectedly, he is overcome by an extraordinary mystical experience:

The Son of Man walked upon the stone walls and intensified the colour of the flowers and quickened the wings of the robin and the little wren. He was at home. With ease he breathed the thin, light air of the heavenly places.

This evokes in him a surrealistic medley of childhood memories, folk-songs, literary characters and even comical incidents at his chapel. Nevertheless he kneels and drinks from the river as if he were taking communion. He is at one with *the green earth* and has gained his inheritance.

Meurig's fantastic vision is purely emotional and has little in common with orthodox religious experience. It might be said that the author is suggesting that personal emotional experiences, however strange, are more meaningful to individuals than intellectual quests for nebulous principles. Whether Gwyn, the anguished intellectual, who is abandoned early in the narrative, will gain his inheritance and realize his artistic ambitions, we shall never know. It appears unlikely.

'Mendio' (*Getting Better*) concerns Glyn who has been taken to a mental hospital after his ship was hit at sea during the war. But in fact Glyn has never felt better; the hospital is *the gateway to heaven*. His nurse, Sali, innocently teases him: *'Boo! Boo! Boo!' she said. Glyn had never heard anything more beautiful in his life.* It is when his mother visits him that his mood changes. He becomes distraught and maniacal: *He held his hand under his mother's chin and two tears fell onto it . . . He licked them like a cat and held out his hand for more.* After a bout of fever he recovers somewhat but, paradoxically, he was a happier man when he was mentally ill: madness has its blessings. He would not then have been expected to fight the war with all its *pain and suffering*. And in that state neither would he have had to confront his mother.

It is this element in the story which gives it an added dimension. The emotional relationship between Glyn and his mother is psychologically complex but, as in the later play HYNT PEREDUR (*Peredur's Progress*), this aspect is not sufficiently developed. Some critics might argue that this is intentional. A psycho-analytical interpretation of Glyn's fantasizing would be intriguing.

The last story in the collection, 'Cerrig y Rhyd' (*The Stepping Stones*) attempts to justify the form and style of the preceding stories. It is also a minutely documented account of a writer's quest for a vision of life.

Absalom, a writer, tells two other characters, Enid and Tomos, that he has written a short story. Enid is also a writer and her reaction is amusingly candid: *I hope that it has a proper plot to it . . . I'm more than sick and tired of these stories that have no structure, which presuppose that an idea and an analysis à la Freud are sufficient to create literature.* She censures Absalom for his *quack philosophizing* and *posturing*.

Absalom welcomes such frank criticism because as a child he had to endure his mother's indifference towards him. As a consequence he decided that the only way to command her attention would be to commit suicide. But his would be no ordinary suicide. Fasting to death or drowning would perhaps only harden his mother's feelings towards him. His death would have to be both *romantic* and *tragic* like Constantin's death in Chekhov's play THE SEAGULL.

However, as he matures, Absalom is able to reject such morbid feelings. No longer is he troubled by his mother's indifference. From the stepping-stones, which symbolize the numerous *deaths* he has considered, he *slips* into the waters of real life. No longer will he wallow in his egotism: he will *dwell . . . in the experiences of others.* At long last he is blessed with *a sense of proportion.*

It is this *sense of proportion* which often saves John Gwilym Jones's characters from utter despair and nihilism. Edwin Lloyd in LLE MYNNO'R GWYNT repeats the phrase as he tries to come to terms with family tragedy; Huw, after his traumas at the end of the play AC ETO NID MYFI, experiences similar feelings; likewise Elwyn – in the novel TRI DIWRNOD AC ANGLADD (*Three Days and a Funeral*) – who, like Absalom, had been emotionally wounded by an aloof and indifferent mother.

In 'Cerrig y Rhyd', Enid's closing remark – *Here, in a few words, is my idea* – is enigmatic. Absalom, at the beginning of the story, admires her ability as a writer to convey her characters' feelings by recording only their outward behaviour: *She can see a husband and wife sitting in their garden on a summer's evening and the girl next door, by means of a word and a seemingly innocent smile, alienating the two from each other.* Is John Gwilym Jones implying that as a writer he himself lacks this unique ability? Or does he expect Enid, in the light of the absorbing self-analysis she has just heard, to retract her early criticism? One can only conclude that the ambiguity is intentional.

The lack of an engaging narrative and the characters' elegant and intense self-analysis in these stories can tax the casual reader's concentration. In an interview with Saunders Lewis in CREFFT Y STORI FER, John Gwilym Jones willingly conceded *that some writers make a virtue of their unintelligibility* but he also maintained that readers are often *lazy, expecting to be given something from one reading.* Y GOEDEN EIRIN is his most consciously modernistic work.

After Y GOEDEN EIRIN, which was published in 1946, John Gwilym Jones published very little prose for more than thirty years. A first chapter for a novel, which he never completed, appeared in the periodical YR ARLOESWR (*The Pioneer*) in 1957, and a short story 'Dyletswydd' (*Duty*) appeared in STORÏAU'R DEFFRO (*Stories of the Awakening*) in 1959. It was 1979 before he published a volume of prose, the novel TRI DIWRNOD AC ANGLADD. But plays were another matter and in 1958 John Gwilym Jones published two in one volume: LLE MYNNO'R GWYNT (*Where the Wind Listeth*) written in 1945, and GŴR LLONYDD (*A Man of Rest*) written in 1953.

LLE MYNNO'R GWYNT deals with the devastating effect of war on the family of Edwin Lloyd. Edwin is a minister who supplements his income by writing English detective novels about the exploits of a certain Sexton Lee, under the pseudonym Calvin Welsh. He is assisted by his wife, Alis. It is she who provides him with ideas and they enjoy what she describes affectionately as a meaningful *symbiotic* relationship. They have four children, Huw, Dewi, Mair and Janet. The writing has not only enabled the couple to provide their children with a sound education – Huw has been to college and Dewi is studying art at the Slade – but has also brought *a sense of proportion* to Edwin's life.

But all is not well. Alis, even at the beginning of the play, is conscious of life's potential tragedy and declares that if she were a poet she would muse not upon *the bliss of the past* nor upon *the glories of the future* but upon *the certainty of the present*. Ironically, it is at this point in the play that we hear from off-stage the voice of a newspaper seller announcing that war is imminent.

The impending war compels the children to confront personal choices. Huw will not join the war because of his pacifism. Yet he cannot decide whether his pacifism is motivated by principle or by an obsessional fear of death. Dewi, the artist, thirsts for an all-encompassing experience of life which will give depth to his paintings:

DEWI: . . . *Being able to realize that this old world is not only pure but also foul, not only welcoming but repulsive, that God and the Devil walk in the garden.*

He experiences such emotions when he walks past an old mill on his way home:

I always adore the place . . . the river unable to push its way through the moss, and the alders with their shining leaves. Tonight, Eban had just finished mucking out the cowshed and the big old cockerel was pecking in the steaming dung-heap. Suddenly, I saw that it was the sum of these things that was beautiful . . . Together they are part of life and in looking at them I feel the thrill of vision.

He yearns for his father's *sense of proportion* but wishes to experience it at a more intense, artistic level.

Dewi's wife, Gwladys, loves him but suggests that her love for him does not necessarily bring happiness in its wake. Were she able to love Huw she might well experience happiness, but she is not attracted to him. She is excited by Dewi's sexuality and courage. She concedes that her feelings are irrational but accepts that life is not governed by reason. Ironically she hopes that someday she can be of comfort to Huw.

Trefor, Janet's boyfriend, is a pragmatist. Despite being an atheist he is convinced that the impending war will be a just one: *All I know is . . . that this diabolical power in Germany today threatens civilization.*

Janet, thrilled by the prospect of marrying Trefor, declares that *this is the happiest night . . . but also the saddest* of her life. She loves her family but ironically she instinctively feels as if she hates someone who is present: before the end of the play she will express her loathing of Huw's pacifism.

Mair's life is meaningless. Bored by her humdrum existence and envious of Janet's apparent happiness, she longs for death: *I have nothing. I hate myself.* Much to Mair's outrage, Janet helps her father to choose a text for his forthcoming sermon at random – with a pin. In the light of the impending mayhem such frivolity is, in Mair's view, sheer blasphemy. But Edwin retorts by asserting that such frivolity provides life with *a sense of proportion.*

Act One ends with Janet reading a poignant verse from St John's Gospel: *The wind bloweth where it listeth, and thou hearest the sound thereof, but canst not tell whence it cometh, and whither it goeth . . .*

Four years have passed by the beginning of Act Two, and the war is at its height. The lives of the characters have been profoundly transformed. Janet and Trefor have lost a child; Huw has become more resentful, morbid and confused, and the war has not enriched Dewi's vision of life as he had hoped. He now *enjoys killing*:

> . . . *Instead of dreading the thought of flying over Germany I crave to see the darkness coming . . . I feel like dancing to the purr of the Lancasters . . . My delight was creating . . . today, it is destruction . . . I have lost my sense of proportion.*

Nevertheless, Gwladys is still attached to him, though she wishes that she could hate him for destroying her happiness.

Mair, the most embittered of the children at the beginning of the play, has become a devout Roman Catholic and has mellowed. No longer does she attempt to live off her *own petty resources; life is far simpler* and she can *draw comfort and strength from the same source as Saint Theresa, Augustine and Saint David.* She believes that her new faith suits her and gives her peace.

The first scene of Act Two ends with a phone call from Janet informing the family that Trefor has been killed. In the second scene the family awaits the arrival of Janet, and the atmosphere is strained. The talk is of personal belief. Huw is still obsessed by a fear of death, and Mair takes him to task for his self-centredness: *You think that your petty life is so important that you cannot bear to think of the world being without it.*

Dewi believes that goodness will conquer some day but *having to die takes the edge off the joy of that conquest.* If he had the imagination to picture such a scenario *death would not be such an anticlimax.* Alas, he is not blessed with the requisite imagination. When Janet does arrive she vents her resentment upon Huw. From now on Janet will *live and live and live to hate.*

Edwin's instinctive reaction is to turn to prayer despite the fact that even prayer is no more than *some marvellous madness . . . the madness that keeps men sane.* It is Huw and Gwladys who voice the prevailing despair:

HUW: *. . . Everybody twisting everything to shape their own little world. My father and mother and Mair deceiving themselves and living in the make-believe land of their faith, Janet making hatred a matter of duty.*
GWLADYS: *And Dewi analysing himself to spiritual and bodily impotence.*

The two declare their love for each other and resolve to build for themselves *a little sanctuary . . . to comfort each other.*

An ecstatic Dewi enters, having experienced momentarily his vision of life:

. . . The sun was setting and casting its redness on the green of the laurel leaves beneath the bedroom window. Suddenly a robin settled upon one of them . . . I saw the two reds . . . the blaze of the sun on the lustrous leaf and the soothing red of the little bird's breast . . . it was like a resurrection.

But, alas, it is only a transient vision.

44

In Act Three, which takes place a year later, Dewi's disillusionment and despair have reached traumatic depths. In his now abstract paintings he strives to reflect a mad world which he cannot come to terms with; he feels that individuals of his kind should be dead. But in Edwin's view his nihilism is a *presumptuous, cynical ungodliness* and for the first and only time in the play Edwin blames himself for his children's despair:

. . . I and people like me have languished in the comfort of our own certainty, of our own faith, without realizing that our children were slipping and slipping. No discipline, not in education, nor religion, nor politics, only the soft lame belief in man's ability to look after himself . . . Creating gods of your senses without ever acknowledging the one God who gave them to you. When you lose them, you have nothing . . . less than nothing.

When Dewi tells Gwladys of his desire to commit suicide, she decides to help him. After his suicide she will marry Huw in the hope that bringing up a family will allay Huw's death-wish. Ironically, at long last both Dewi and Gwladys understand each other:

DEWI: You are giving me the thing I yearned for.
GWLADYS: And experiencing the thing I yearned for.
DEWI: Quite!

In the last scene Huw and Gwladys are about to leave for Canada. Gwladys had intended to stay to try to *challenge Dewi's presence* but has decided to *begin everything anew.* Alis, aware of Gwladys's role in Dewi's suicide, declares bitterly that she *never wants to see her again* and *has prayed . . . that they will never have children.* But immediately she regrets having said this. She hopes that Gwladys will *leave Dewi at home* with her. This is Gwladys's sincerest wish too and it is she who gives voice to the play's predominant theme:

GWLADYS: *Everything was inevitable?*
ALIS LLOYD: *Do you think so?*
GWLADYS: *If it hadn't been a war, it would have been something else. Nobody can run away from his own nature.*

The end is not wholly pessimistic. Edwin has come across one of Huw's old school copy-books. He hopes that his son's innocent and somewhat waggish attempts at creative writing will inspire their children someday. When Gwladys and Huw have left, it is Edwin, who has been blessed with a *a sense of proportion*, who witnesses *a thrush making its nest in the garden hedge*. Alis too will have her memories of Dewi to comfort her:

ALIS LLOYD: (smiling with joy) *She left him here for me.*
EDWIN LLOYD: *Left him?*
ALIS LLOYD: *Dewi, Edwin.* (looking at her husband) *He is still here.*

This is not only a play about a family crisis but also a play about how individuals choose to come to terms with such a crisis. As John Rowlands points out in DYRNAID O AWDURON CYFOES, the family members opt for solutions appropriate to their own personalities, and it is not reason which governs their actions but instinct. No one viewpoint is regarded as being morally superior to another: Dewi's desire for a comprehensive vision of life is treated as sympathetically as Mair's conversion to Catholicism, and Huw's pacifism is not offered as a superior alternative to Trefor's commitment to the principle of a just war. If one had to single out one individual for whom the playwright has a degree of sympathy it would be Edwin Lloyd who strives amidst the confusion for some kind of stability. It is he who strikes a note of optimism at the end.

Gwennan Tomos has argued convincingly that the characters in the earlier plays attempt to struggle against fate, whilst in this play they appear to resign themselves to the inevitable. However, it is significant that Janet, the one and only character who experiences a real and profound personal tragedy, takes leave of the family and does not appear at all in Act Three. Could it be that the playwright's all-forgiving humanism cannot come to terms with the sheer magnitude of her tragedy and her subsequent contempt for life itself?

This extremely intense play perhaps at times makes undue demands on a theatre audience – and the word 'theatre' is relevant in this context. In an early review of John Gwilym Jones's work, the playwright John Ellis Williams, criticized this play's unremitting wordiness and its overt intellectualism. Only rarely is the audience given respite from the characters' passionate self-analysis. Elan Closs Stephens has rightly drawn attention to the fact that the play has too many principal characters, which compounds this problem for the audience. One could also forgive an audience for occasionally confusing Dewi's crisis with that of his brother Huw, because of the similarity of tone which is apparent in their intellectual musings. We hear not the 'spoken thought' of the characters but the voice of the dramatist.

Again, it is the artist's thirst for inner tranquillity – in this case, a poet's – which is the central theme of GŴR LLONYDD. Poli Lewis is a widow with four children: Glyn, Pyrs, Robin and Beti. Her ageing father, Richard Gruffydd, a retired minister, lives with the family. In the opening scenes of Act One we are made aware of the decline of the traditional religious culture in post-1945 Wales. Beti, the rather breezy but likeable younger daughter, argues with her mother about the propriety of visiting the seaside on a Sunday. The apparent generation gap is accentuated when Richard Gruffydd enters maundering about the past:

R. GRUFFYDD: I'll be late . . . I'll be late. I was late at the chapel only once.
MRS LEWIS: Dad, there's nearly an hour before it's time for chapel.
R. GRUFFYDD: Only once. I remember well. There was a Preaching Meeting at Sardis Llanegwyl. It was midsummer and I had just happened to fall asleep after tea and those stupid chapel-house people forgot to wake me up and there I was running up the hill and the presiding elder, old John Williams, Hafod, at the chapel door, livid and shouting at the top of his voice, 'Hurry up you . . . a chapel full of people waiting for you and you're dragging your feet.'

Martha, an old friend of Mrs Lewis, arrives with her daughter, Sidi. They have left the village and now live in London. Having witnessed the decline in attendance at the chapel that Sunday morning she is demoralized. Her disquiet is echoed by Mrs Lewis, who reluctantly concedes that her own children are more preoccupied with their own personal problems than with chapel life.

Pyrs, a student, is a cynic who has not only rejected

his upbringing but also the nationalist aspirations of his generation:

MRS LEWIS: . . . He never takes anything seriously . . . laughing at everything . . . Many a time I've begged him to go and help at the 'Aelwyd' when he's home on holiday like this . . . or become a hard-working member of Plaid Cymru. 'Mam, Wales isn't worth saving,' he says, 'and if she were, what's the point? Some day there will be nothing of her left except a mushroom cloud hovering above.'

Pyrs's philosophy of life is deterministic:

PYRS: Only a complete idiot, someone utterly ignorant, hopes to change the future. It has been determined from the beginning. The only sensible thing to do is to ignore everything and live from day to day without a care for tomorrow . . .

Glyn has been badly wounded in the war. A winner of the Crown at the National Eisteddfod, he has recently published a volume of poetry. Despite his disability it appears that he is happily married to Megan and has not become embittered:

GLYN: Here am I, thirty years old, a helpless cripple at the mercy of a mother, a wife and two crutches.
MRS LEWIS: Surely you're not feeling sorry for yourself.
GLYN: Not at all . . . I enjoy living a full and contented life on the kindness and experiences of other people . . . living on my own thoughts as Sidi was so quick to realize. Nothing to do except listen to the radio . . . and read and read . . . write a little every now and then . . . and imagine.

The other son, Robin, is something of an enigma. Five years previously he left home *without a word of explanation . . . without even a handshake* in the middle of his college studies. But, despite his absence, and the fact that his mother *never utters his name*, he is omnipresent. Whatever the reason for his hasty departure, Glyn feels that he should be forgiven, especially by his mother. But widowhood has turned their mother into a hard woman:

MRS LEWIS: There is this notion that love is boundless . . . everlasting . . . but I'm not sure. Your father has been dead for fifteen years . . . you four were children. If I remember rightly I did love him but by now I can think about him somewhat uncaringly and on Palm Sunday I can place a posy of primroses on his grave in as uninvolved a manner as I wash down the doorstep.

But Glyn has only admiration for his brother Robin. He too was a poet, and at one time the better poet. Not only were his senses keener, but he possessed an unusual Keatsian-like *capacity to idle away creatively* and experience *life-giving introspection*.

At the end of the first scene we learn from Megan that Robin has returned home and the reason for his hasty departure soon becomes apparent. It transpires that Robin and Megan have had an affair but this affair, much to Megan's disappointment, had been in Robin's words no more than a poet's yearning for *novel experiences*. Until recently he had been full of guilt, to such an extent that he had lost his *capacity to idle away creatively*. No longer at peace with himself, and no longer, as he himself admits, *a man of rest*, he is unable to write poetry. But whilst attending chapel in London he came *face to face with something within himself which [was] clean and pure*. Now that he has met Sidi, Martha's daughter, and is about to marry her, he yearns to rid himself of *sin and guilt* in order to regain his *former contentment*. He intends to inform

Glyn of the affair. Megan is exasperated by Robin's selfishness:

MEGAN: And to regain your former contentment you're prepared to put Glyn and me through hell.
ROBIN: You don't understand.
MEGAN: I understand too well. You come home and open old wounds . . . you talk of your sin and your guilt and your chapel and your Sidi as though nothing existed apart from yourself.

The scene between Robin, Megan and Glyn is arguably the most carefully written and constructed in the entire play. When Megan informs Glyn that Robin had asked Martha not to tell their mother about the marriage, the ensuing exchange is laden with irony:

GLYN: . . . Well, there's nothing like confessing . . . Robin, I'm very happy . . . a girl who can understand you just like Megan understands me . . . but it will be a happier life for her than for Megan.
ROBIN: I read your book.
GLYN: With Sidi?
ROBIN: Yes . . . together.
GLYN: I'll never be a great poet like you.
ROBIN: I'll be a silent poet for ever if I don't.
GLYN: If you don't what?
MEGAN: Why won't you be a great poet, Glyn?
GLYN: Because I can't be still in the right way, like Robin can.
ROBIN: I don't understand.
GLYN: My world is far too secure. My stillness arises from my sense of certainty that nothing disturbing can happen to me.
ROBIN: But disturbing things can happen to you . . things that you never imagined.
MEGAN: A cigarette, Robin?

The irony intensifies when Pyrs enters musing about Sidi with whom he has become infatuated. Robin's presence is about to shatter not only Glyn's cherished contentment but also his cynical brother's new-found joy.

Act Two takes place three days later. The significant exchange is that between Pyrs and Megan during which Pyrs confesses that he has come to terms with his disappointment; indeed his fleeting infatuation with Sidi has allayed his cynicism and has given him new hope: *If a moment like that was possible three days ago, it could happen to me again.*

But Megan is preoccupied with Robin's intentions and Pyrs is sympathetic:

PYRS: Did you love Robin?
MEGAN: Love him? I don't know. The only thing I know is that I had no defences against him (challenging him). *And none of you has the right to blame me for not having any . . .*
PYRS: I'm not blaming you, Megan.

Later that night, Megan is about to divulge her innermost feelings to Glyn but they are interrupted by Robin and she leaves. It is at this point that Glyn, having been reassured of Megan's love, rebukes Robin for suggesting that Megan should have been given an opportunity to confess:

ROBIN: Sharing her pain . . . confessing. . . would alleviate the pain.

Glyn rejects this notion: *It would . . . make her cowardly, selfish rather than brave . . . and show that she was too weak to stand the pain.* But Robin claims that poets attain greatness by sharing their pain with others. This notion too is refuted by Glyn. Poets like himself attempt to *share their pain with humanity* not with other individuals. Candour in everyday life can be perilous.

Robin, whom Glyn had assumed was *a man of rest* but whose return has precipitated restlessness and guilt within the family, leaves for London a more enlightened and less selfish man. He has perhaps gained his *former quietness* and is once more *a man of rest*.

It is unfortunate from a purely dramatic point of view that Megan and Glyn are allowed to touch upon the affair during the last scene, as it tends to undermine Glyn's observations in the previous scene. None the less Glyn is given an opportunity to confess his own failings: *Whatever your body did, my mind did exactly the same thing many a time.* To seek each other's forgiveness would be an act of sheer smugness. Their only recourse is to try to forget the past. After all, the passing of time has enabled their mother to come to terms with their father's death. The play appears to end on an optimistic note.

But is this in fact the case? At the end of the play, Poli Lewis is bewildered by this inexplicable human capacity to forget the past. When her senile father, who is so obsessed with punctuality throughout the play, appears to have forgotten about the evening's *seiat* meeting at the chapel she gives vent to her anxieties:

MRS LEWIS: (really agitated) *Dad, don't you forget . . . ever . . . ever . . . I couldn't bear that. Everything and everybody changing . . . don't you change . . .*

And how are we to interpret Megan's guarded response to Glyn's compassion and optimism in the closing scene?

GLYN: *Before long all this will be totally insignificant.*
MEGAN: *Yes . . .*
GLYN: *And I'll still be asking more of you than any human being has the right to do.*
MEGAN: *No . . .*

Does she suspect him of concealing his true feelings? Is she poignantly conscious of his inner anguish which she will never be allowed to allay? In the light of Glyn's earlier observations about the artist's fate, her suspicions are perhaps not unwarranted. Despite appearing to be the true *man of rest*, Glyn, the crippled compassionate poet, will perhaps never attain inner tranquillity.

Although the title comes from a verse in the First Book of Chronicles in which David tells his son Solomon, that he *shall be a man of rest* through whom God *will give peace and quietness unto Israel in his days,* conventional religion plays no part in Glyn's vision. It is an existentialist vision: it is he who gives meaning to his own existence. Richard Gruffydd does indeed symbolize changelessness in the play but he also symbolizes the decay and irrelevance of traditional religion.

Y TAD A'R MAB (*The Father and the Son*), written in 1959 and revised before its publication in 1963, concerns an individual who has not been blessed with a *sense of proportion* and as a consequence is unable to restrain his innermost impulses. Richard Owen, an insurance office manager, is married to

Casi and they have two sons, Elis and Gwyn. Elis, an easygoing joiner, is the elder and is about to marry his fiancée Lora, whilst Gwyn, the more bookish of the two, is at school studying for a scholarship examination. Once each of the characters has been introduced by 'The Voice', a chorus-like character taking on the role of inquisitive neighbour, the action commences.

The atmosphere is ostensibly relaxed. Casi is about to leave with Elis and Lora to see their new house and Gwyn, much to Casi's disapproval, is playing darts. It is when Richard Owen's name is mentioned that one infers that all is not well:

ELIS: *You don't know my father as he used to be, does she, Mam?*
CASI: (trying to avoid giving an answer) *Mm?*
ELIS: *Lora doesn't know my father as he used to be, before . . .*
CASI: *Before what?*
ELIS: *Before whatever has happened to him . . . happened.*

Gwyn is too preoccupied with his dart-playing to respond to their concern about his father:

GWYN: *Mam, do you see the bull?*
CASI: (without understanding) *What bull?*
LORA: *He means the exact centre of the board.*
GWYN: *Yes, the still centre as Morgan Llwyd puts it.*
CASI: *Well, what about it?*
GWYN: *I won't be satisfied until I reach it.*

This reference to the *still centre* is symbolic. The phrase brings to mind the religious philosophy of the seventeenth-century Welsh Puritan, Morgan Llwyd. It is a phrase used to describe a yearned-for inner tranquillity, in Llwyd's case a spiritual union with God.

Gwyn's relationship with his father is frustrated by a normal adolescent craving for romantic experiences. Ironically, it is Elis's seemingly innocent promptings that set the tragedy in motion:

ELIS: *Gwyn, tell me. Have you ever been out with a girl?*
GWYN: (slowly) *No.*
ELIS: *Well, you ought to. The sooner the better. Why not tonight? As soon as the house is empty out you go.*

Eventually Richard Owen arrives home and demands to know what Elis has been telling Gwyn, and an argument ensues. It is at this point in Act One that Richard Owen's peculiar ambitions for his son are made clear:

RICHARD OWEN: *Listen, if you win this scholarship, I shall feel exactly the same as if I'd won it myself, and if you fail I shall feel as if I had failed myself. I'm as close to you as that. Everything that happens to you happens to me. I can't think of myself existing apart from you.*

When Richard Owen, encouraged by Gwyn, leaves to join the others, Gwyn seizes the opportunity to introduce himself to their new neighbours' daughter Pegi, a spirited, unreserved and intelligent young girl who works at a local factory. Gwyn's amorous overtures are amusingly inept but at times the exchange between them has ominous overtones:

GWYN: *There's no one at home.*
PEGI: *What would your father and mother say?*
GWYN: *Mother wouldn't say anything.*
PEGI: *And your father?*

GWYN: *He doesn't suffer from lack of words.*
PEGI: *He'd tear my hair out.*
GWYN: *Shouldn't be surprised.*

On their return home Casi pulls a muscle outside the house and Pegi, much to Richard Owen's irritation, helps her inside. The family, including Richard Owen, does not suspect that Gwyn has already met Pegi. It is when Gwyn insists on escorting Pegi home that Richard Owen suspects that something is afoot:

GWYN: (challenging his father) *I'll see you home all the same. (*to Pegi*) Come along.*
PEGI: *Don't let it worry you too much Mr Owen, I'll look after him.*
R.O.: *How did she know that I was Mr Owen?*
CASI: (not having heard) *Mmm?*
R.O.: (louder and nastier) *How did she know my name?*

But it appears that Richard Owen should not have been unduly concerned about Gwyn. At the beginning of Act Two, Gwyn is disenchanted not so much with Pegi, but with himself. He is unaccustomed to witnessing physical manifestations of love and has displayed little if any enthusiasm for the normal physical side of their relationship. This irritates Pegi.

GWYN: . . . *I never saw my father kissing my mother. I would feel most uncomfortable if I did.*
PEGI: *More's the pity.*

But the experience has nevertheless been worthwhile for Gwyn:

GWYN: *You have given me something that I never had before . . . a sort of trust. I am contented . . . no longer restless or unhappy . . . I have no trouble in concentrating completely on my work . . . I sleep well every night.*

Gwyn's object of affection in life can only be his father:

GWYN: . . . Honestly, there is nothing in the world I want more than to be able to satisfy him – to give myself to him and hear him say that he's satisfied. One day I will hear him say that. . . and it will be like . . .
PEGI: Like what?
GWYN: Like a baptism.

Pegi, to Gwyn's relief, agrees to tell Richard Owen *that he needn't worry about his little boy.* They resolve to be no more than friends.

Unaware of this, Richard Owen is becoming more and more convinced that Pegi has a destructive influence on Gwyn:

R.O.: Just look at her . . .
CASI: She's a nice enough girl.
R.O.: The whore!
CASI: Richard.
R.O.: A dirty, filthy little whore.

In his eyes Gwyn is no ordinary child:

R.O.: [God] will use him for his own purpose. But the way must be prepared and the way must be made straight . . . That is my task . . . And when the day comes I shall be able to hand him over, I shall say 'Here he is, take thou him'.
CASI: To his death.
R.O.: Death?
CASI: That is what happened to that other son.
R.O.: Which son?

Unknown to the family Richard Owen has written to Pegi threatening to kill her. Elis inadvertently discovers this letter, but again Richard Owen justifies his actions, drawing disturbing biblical parallels:

R.O.: . . . That was the only way to save him. We've all had to make sacrifices for his sake . . . That's the way God works in the world. The wanton wickedness of Jezebel and the unbelief of the prophets of Baal were necessary to make Elijah a man of God. It was when Judas betrayed him and Peter denied him that Jesus Christ was able to prove that he was the Son of God . . .

In the meantime, Pegi has promised Gwyn that she will tell his father that their affair is over. But when confronted by this troubled family she decides not to do so; instead, she is overwhelmed by sheer mischief:

PEGI: . . . I wonder what you'd look like in a grey silk hat, Gwyn?

Richard Owen is enraged by her effrontery:

R.O.: You won't marry my son while you have breath left in your body. Do you hear? While you have a breath left in your body. And now, leave my house.

But Pegi tells them that she has received a threatening letter, although she has not informed the police. She departs somewhat cockily, leaving the family to brood upon their predicament.

The opening scene of Act Three underlines the effect which Richard Owen's actions have had on Elis and Lora. Their wedding plans will have to be postponed *until things have quietened down*. Elis's inability to face up to the crisis exasperates Lora:

LORA: *They will never quieten down without facing the facts Elis. You are being just like your father. If he had faced the fact that a boy of eighteen isn't a boy any longer we would not be in this wretched mess. You are being just as evasive.*

Gwyn, too, is behaving *like a stubborn idiot*; after the affair of the letter he is refusing to tell his father that Pegi means *nothing to him*. Lora insists that Gwyn should be told of the vile contents of the first letter regardless of the possible effect on his performance in the impending scholarship examination. When Gwyn is told, he finds himself unable to accept that his father would carry out such a deed:

GWYN: *. . . My father would never think of such a thing. He is a good man. A very good man.*
LORA: *And you'll tell him that, won't you Gwyn?*
GWYN: *Can't you see . . . you blind fools, can't you see? I love him . . . I love him . . .*

Casi returns home and informs Gwyn and Elis that she has left Richard alone in the park. The two boys immediately decide to look for him. Casi is under the impression that the boys are afraid that Richard might commit suicide, but she is not intimidated by such a prospect. There is a suggestion that she would be willing to let things take their course:

CASI: *Afraid he would do himself harm?*
LORA: *Yes, perhaps.*
CASI: *I suppose that there are worse things than doing harm to yourself.*
LORA: *Yes, there are.*

Nevertheless, Casi and Lora decide to join in the search.

60

Richard Owen arrives home, alone. He appears at peace with himself and he begins to play darts. When Gwyn arrives before the rest of the family he is relieved to see his father so composed:

R.O.: *Look at my hand.* (He holds it in front of him.) *It's as steady as a rock. When your mind is still, at rest, your limbs are also steady.*
GWYN: *Yes.*
R.O.: *And your mind is at ease always when you are sure that you are doing the right thing* (he shows his hand and draws his finger along the lifeline). *They tell me that this is the lifeline. This one that circles the cushion of your thumb.*
GWYN: *Yours is long, father.*
R.O.: *It reaches the back of my hand.*
GWYN: *That means you will live for ever, father.*

Gwyn's sole desire from now on is to please his father:

GWYN: *I will do everything in my power to please you, father, and make you well pleased with me.*
R.O.: (almost crying) *Gwyn, my dear boy.*

At last he confesses that Pegi means nothing to him; he became involved with Pegi because he *wanted to know what was happening outside [his] father's world.* Now, after this experience, Gwyn has his own vision of life:

. . . Good and bad belong very closely to each other. Very often you can't tell which is which . . . The same action can be good on one occasion and evil on another. That's what Pegi taught me. Sometimes when I kissed her it was hateful, it made me hate myself, lose my self-respect; another time, it was something beautiful, full of the joy of living. But again and again something which began by being beautiful would slowly slide

into something repulsive. It happens with everything. It's people like us who create good and evil by the way we look at the things we do . . .

Gwyn can even sympathize with his father's motives for writing the letters:

GWYN: Yes, I understand that you had to. But you thought that you were doing the right thing. You believed that everything that came between us was evil and unclean . . . and you had to . . . destroy it. You didn't see anything wrong in that . . .

After this intimate scene the tension between the father and son appears to have been relieved:

GWYN: (holds him tightly to comfort him) There you are, father, everything will be all right, everything will be all right now.

For a brief moment, Gwyn appears to have at last arrived at the *still centre* and is experiencing that deep emotional union with his father for which he yearned.

When Casi and Lora return, they too are relieved to see Richard Owen. But their relief is short-lived; Elis arrives with a policeman. Richard Owen has murdered Pegi.

The power of the play derives from its sound structure. Gwennan Tomos contends that all the characters, like those in Greek tragedy, unwittingly play a role in the hero's downfall. It is not only Gwyn's obstinacy and Pegi's mischief that precipitate the catastrophe: Casi, because of her passive nature, is unwilling to accept that parental love and ambition have degenerated into a perverse kind of Messianism. It is Elis, the most carefree and innocent of all the characters, who encourages Gwyn to seek a girlfriend in the first place. Like Creon in Sophocles' ANTIGONE, Richard Owen attempts to save his son from a woman and, in so doing, destroys his 'house'. In this play it is not the curse of the gods which predetermines the tragedy but the inaction of flawed personalities.

The Owen family is also a product of a particular environment and culture but Pegi, despite living in the same street, belongs to a different culture. She is a product of an emerging secularism which threatens to undermine traditional Nonconformist values. Thus, today's audience is poignantly conscious of an additional irony in the play. Richard Owen, in attempting to save Gwyn, is also attempting to safeguard the aspirations of a particular culture which is embodied by Gwyn. But arguably this culture was beginning to disintegrate and decay at the time the play was written. His actions appear to us, today, to be as ironic as those of Creon and Antigone who, in their different ways, attempt to save a 'house' already cursed.

In his book ANTIGONES, the critic George Steiner states that the *Greek tragic chorus is a matchlessly supple instrument* and that its *role in the play can vary between utter involvement and indifference*. In Y TAD A'R MAB, 'The Voice', whose role has often been compared to that of a Greek chorus, does not involve itself directly in the fate of the characters. Throughout the play, it is aware of the impending tragedy but does not intervene. Could it be that this seemingly benign character is in fact the embodiment of those indifferent, cruel and unaccountable forces which determine an individual's fate?

This play also has an intriguing religious dimension which calls for further exploration. It has already been argued that Richard Owen's parental aspirations are a form of perverse Messianism. This suggests that perhaps the playwright expects his audience to question and challenge the very notion of Messianism – the belief that an individual has been chosen for a profound mission in life. The implication here is that Messianism can be either benign or destructive, depending on the make-up of the individuals concerned. In this instance, because of Richard Owen's disturbed personality, this belief becomes corrupted and leads to evil.

Thus, if principles or beliefs or doctrines, however righteous they may appear, are at the mercy of individual personality, would it not be wiser to reject them and seek in life what is truly meaningful? John Gwilym Jones would explore this question in his next major play.

HANES RHYW GYMRO (*A Welshman's Story*) written in 1964, was conceived after he saw a performance of John Osborne's LUTHER in London. In Osborne's play, itself inspired by Brecht's THE LIFE OF GALILEO, Martin Luther is portrayed as a man consumed by inner conflicts resulting from his theological convictions. Osborne also suggests that Luther's public recalcitrance is induced by a more mundane personal affliction. One critic aptly described Osborne's Luther as *driven from within, with the secret cause literally working away in his bowels*. It was Osborne's preoccupation with the motivation and emotions of a major historical figure that prompted John Gwilym Jones to search Welsh history for an individual whom he could explore in a similar vein. He chose Morgan Llwyd, the seventeenth-century Puritan. This is hardly surprising: he had always been fascinated by Llwyd and there are numerous references to him in his earlier works.

The central theme of HANES RHYW GYMRO is more specific than that of LUTHER. In an interview with Gwyn Thomas in MABON, John Gwilym Jones argues that it is not intellectual convictions that dictate the action of individuals but rather the *personal emotional relationship between man and man*. In his opinion, Llwyd's life as he *knew and interpreted* it was *a fitting example of this principle*.

Llwyd lived in an age of extraordinary political and intellectual change. Individuals were not only overwhelmed by a feeling of confusion at seeing the destruction of an existing order – the execution of Charles I and the coming to power of Cromwell – but also bewildered by a plethora of competing theological viewpoints which presumed to offer answers, if not indeed, absolute truths. The prevalent belief that Christ was about to return and reign for a thousand years – millenarianism – gave added urgency to this quest for absolutes.

Act One begins with the young Morgan leaving Cynfal, the family home in the Merioneth parish of Maentwrog, to attend school in Wrexham. It appears that he is reluctant to leave. The relationship between him and his grandfather Huw Cynfal, an accomplished poet, is close and meaningful. Their love of *cynghanedd* (Welsh alliterative poetry in the strict metres) and its attendant lore is in sharp contrast to the pious Anglicanism of his mother. In these early scenes there are intimations of the impending religious tensions which will eventually overwhelm Morgan. He is first presented with a BOOK OF COMMON PRAYER by his mother; then Huw Cynfal, who has not wholly abandoned Roman Catholicism, presents him with a crucifix belonging to a distant relative John Roberts, a Catholic martyr. When Siencyn Dafydd, the good-natured battle-scarred mercenary who is to accompany him to Wrexham, unashamedly confesses to changing his military loyalties in the light of political expediency, Morgan is perplexed:

MORGAN: What about principle?
SIENCYN: Mog, lad, you'll live to a ripe old age to see principle on one side and no principle on the other.

Despite their different outlooks and personalities, Morgan and Siencyn are inseparable, although Morgan's loyalty to Siencyn will eventually be put to the test.

In his quest for spiritual certainty Morgan is moved by the preaching of the Puritan Walter Cradoc. He decides to follow Cradoc, but he is still dogged by uncertainty and conflicting emotions. It is Siencyn who consoles him:

MORGAN: O Siencyn, what's happening to me? What's happening to me? I'm afraid . . . afraid. Hold me Siencyn, hold me tightly.
(Siencyn embraces him and rocks him as if he were a baby.)
SIENCYN: That's it Morgan . . . that's it my boy . . .

66

Act Two begins with Llwyd, by now married with children, having joined the *gathered* congregation at Llanfaches, Monmouthshire. His wife Ann is supportive of his evangelizing but at heart longs for a normal relationship:

ANN: Yes . . . yes, of course . . . it's a fact that you're God's prophet . . . But the flesh is also fact . . . your flesh and my flesh. Our son in your arms proves that . . .

These conflicting loyalties are highlighted in a scene where Morgan begins to recite one of his hymns to his son, Dafydd. Siencyn's reaction is amusingly predictable: *Mog, lad, who do you think you've got in your arms? Martin Luther?* Siencyn sings Dafydd a folk-song and eventually Morgan joins in the merriment, but it is short-lived; Vavasor Powell, another Puritan, appears and informs the family that the Civil War has started. Again Morgan's loyalties are put to the test:

ANN: (getting up) I'll go and get things ready.
MORGAN: (silently, firmly) You're not to come, Ann.
ANN: (as if struck) Not to come?
MORGAN: A family is a responsibility. I have a responsibility to God also.
ANN: (bitterly) Are the two different?
MORGAN: Yes, sometimes. In the midst of war I cannot look after you and Dafydd and serve God at the same time.
SIENCYN: (angrily) He's a peculiar kind of God.
MORGAN: Yes, Siencyn, a very peculiar God.

Vavasor Powell at first appears to be a tolerant man but as the war progresses he becomes increasingly belligerent and admires Cromwell's ruthlessness: *Blood was congealing on his throat, but back he went and lunged at the king's pikemen until their coats were red in their own blood.* Morgan has deep misgivings about Powell: *You delight in the pain of others . . . you who prayed to God to put a stop to cruelty;* but Powell, the uncompromising fundamentalist, justifies the cruelty by referring to biblical precedents which Morgan, still under Cradoc's influence, repudiates. Indeed, at this point in the play, Morgan appears to have no viewpoint of his own. When challenged by Powell to explain his beliefs he shouts in anguish: *I don't know! O my God, I don't know,* and in a poignant prayer reveals his true yearnings:

O God, give me my own voice. Instead of listening and listening and reading and reading give within me the ability to speak and write your words.

The action moves to Montgomery and the year is 1644. Morgan is about to preach to the troops before the battle for the town. Before the fighting starts he is introduced to a young soldier, Huw William, from his native parish, Maentwrog. Ironically, they talk not about the impending battle nor about profound theological issues but rather about Morgan's child, Dafydd, whom Huw knows well:

SOLDIER 1: . . . *You're Morgan Llwyd?*
MORGAN: Yes.
SOLDIER 1: *Little Deio's father?*
MORGAN: (nearly crying) *Yes . . .*
SIENCYN: *Is he talking by now?*
SOLDIER: *Babbling everything.*
SIENCYN: (mischievously) *So he takes after his father, Mog?*

This short but intimate exchange prompts Morgan to preach a subdued sermon on the perils of dogmatism and the certainty of God's salvation.

But Morgan's ideals are soon to be found wanting. In a poignant scene, which underlines the central theme of the play, Siencyn is mortally wounded and his last wish is that Morgan should make the sign of the cross over him with a relic. Despite his love for Siencyn his principles prevent him from fulfilling this seemingly innocent wish. Unknown to Siencyn, it is Huw William who does so out of sheer humanity. Outraged and disillusioned by Morgan's lack of compassion, he decides to return home to Maentwrog.

It is Vavasor Powell's belief in Christ's imminent Second Coming, and his belief that a Parliament of Saints will be gathered to serve Christ, which motivates Morgan to continue with his mission. Cradoc however, cannot accept that God will share his sovereignty with factious mortals: *In this world it is men who have to govern . . . good men . . . saints, if you like . . . but yet men of flesh and blood. People like you and me, Morgan, who have to disagree with each other.* Their conflicting viewpoints cause a rift between Morgan and his former mentor. Cradoc no longer plays an active role in the plot and his presence in Act Three is merely symbolic.

This Act begins with the execution of Charles I in 1649. Morgan persuades himself that it is a just act, *a necessity.* He is moved to express this in verse:

> *The law was ever above kings*
> *And Christ above the law.*
> *Unhappy Charles provoked the Lamb*
> *To dust he must withdraw.*

After this self-righteous apologia a weary tramp

appears and muses cynically upon the excesses and hypocrisy of the times:

No, I don't deny that something had to be done. Oliver Cromwell and his Parliament were right there . . . But, God, I can't help thinking sometimes that they too would be wise to shut up. Is getting drunk worse in the long run than what Oliver Cromwell's soldiers did after Naseby? Killing women . . . and that's true, I was there . . . Slashing their faces with sharp knives and singing 'Praise the Lord' at the same time . . .

When at long last Cromwell nominates the Parliament of Saints both Morgan and Powell are ecstatic:

MORGAN: . . . At last! At last! The day of the Lord is dawning . . . The great Sabbath is near. Let all the people shout 'Hosanna'.

Inspired by the prospect of the Second Coming, he completes his classic 'Llythur ir Cymru Cariadus' (*A Letter to the Beloved Welsh People*), an impassioned plea to his fellow Welshmen to prepare themselves for this momentous event. But Ann, his wife, is more concerned with the practicalities of everyday life:

ANN: And I have to bring up your four children.
MORGAN: I know that, but . . .
ANN: (Interrupting him. She has picked up his manuscript.) 'A Letter to the Beloved Welsh People.' Beloved Welsh people . . . I often think that your Welsh are more beloved to you than your own family.

Morgan catches a momentary glimpse of his former self being mesmerized by Cradoc when he is visited by an admirer, John ap John. John even repeats the exact words which Morgan once used to Cradoc, but

Morgan's response, unlike Cradoc's, is restrained:

JOHN AP JOHN: I am going to be a saint like you are a saint.
*MORGAN: (*his mind far away*) Really?*

When John inadvertently calls him Mog, Morgan senses that perhaps he has found not only a kindred spirit intellectually but someone who could be *close, close to him.* John and Deio are instructed to seek out the Quaker George Fox, to learn more about his teachings. At long last it appears that Morgan is a contented soul:

*MORGAN: (*He's quieter, more certain of himself, more peaceful that he has been before.*) Ann, I haven't been so happy since I was a lad at Cynfal. At last everything is as if it were in my favour.*

But his contentment is shattered when a letter arrives from Powell informing him that Cromwell has dissolved the Parliament of Saints. Morgan is devastated and bereft of words.

In the penultimate scene Cradoc and Powell debate the rightfulness of Cromwell's action. Both men plead for Morgan's support for their individual *opinions*, but he rejects their pleas. His religious vision is otherwordly, mystic yet compassionate:

MORGAN: . . . Of what value are opinions and debates face to face with the Almighty God? They are the fire of hell. Both of you approach the Great Nothingness . . . The good wise man lives a life of uncertainty, daily searching and groping, with God looking upon his weakness with mercy . . .

Morgan hopes he can share this vision with people like John ap John but even he – by now a committed

Quaker – rejects Morgan on the grounds that he accepts tithes, a contentious issue in those and later times. At the end of the play a disillusioned Morgan has only his family. He picks up his baby and sings the song Siencyn sang to Deio in an earlier scene. The final stage direction is significant: *(The play ends on a happy, affectionate, tranquil note.)*

The play has been criticized for the way it depicts Llwyd's life. Despite their different personalities there is scant evidence to suggest that the rift between Morgan Llwyd and Vavasor Powell was as deep as that portrayed in the play. M. Wynn Thomas, in his masterly study of Llwyd's life and works (MORGAN LLWYD: EI GYFEILLION A'I GYFNOD, 1991), states that Llwyd *continued to like his old teacher until the end and respected his firm spiritual character.* However, it does appear that his relationship with Powell had from the beginning been fraught with tensions because of their differing personalities; Powell seems to have been the more *violent-tempered and combative* of the two, according to M. Wynn Thomas. There was a difference of opinion between them, but it concerned a more mundane issue, namely state-supported clergy, a system which Powell opposed.

M. Wynn Thomas does suggest that Llwyd had become a disillusioned man towards the end of his short life. But whether his disillusionment was as agonizing as that shown in the last scene is debatable. The nihilism which overcomes Llwyd in the play is arguably the nihilism of modern man searching in vain for metaphysical truths. Indeed, John Gwilym Jones in conversation with his friends, always maintained that this Llwyd was his own

72

creation. As R. Geraint Gruffydd concedes in the CYFROL DEYRNGED, after casting doubt upon the playwright's central thesis and also drawing attention to minor historical inaccuracies, *it is the vision that is important not the history.*

Morgan's dialogue, monologues and sermons in the play echo words, phrases and images taken from his published work. For example, in the opening monologue an audience versed in Llwyd's work will appreciate the allusions to LLYFR Y TRI ADERYN (*The Book of the Three Birds*) in which a raven represents the Anglican clergy, a dove the saints and an eagle God's elected leader, Cromwell:

The place is flocking with birds – ravens in their thousands, croaking, croaking . . . And doves . . . I don't much like killing them although grandad calls them noisy monotonous old creatures, leaving their droppings everywhere. And I'm sure I saw an eagle the other day.

Such meticulous writing commands our admiration but, if one is acquainted with Llwyd's work, there is at times a danger of its appearing too contrived, and therefore of alienating the audience.

Because Osborne's LUTHER was inspired by Brecht's concept of the 'epic theatre' it is often asserted that HANES RHYW GYMRO is the first attempt by a Welsh playwright at writing a Brechtian play. However, despite the play's episodic structure and its use of other Brechtian devices such as first person narrations, the similarity is tenuous. If it is compared with some of Brecht's definitions of epic theatre in his notes on the opera, *The Rise and Fall of the City of Mahagonny*, it is clear that the play does not attempt to arouse the spectator's capacity for political action. As a character, Llwyd is not 'alterable' in the sense that he is prompted by a novel view of his existence to attempt to reform the existing order. Indeed, it is his inherent inability to identify himself with individuals who want to do just that, which is the central theme of the play. In the last scene he has not 'altered' or progressed intellectually but rather has reverted nihilistically to an existence blissfully devoid of intellectual thought. He embraces a simple and uncomplicated life as a solution to his intellectual impasse.

The emphasis is not, as is the case in Brechtian epic theatre, on 'reason' but on 'feeling', a characteristic of the traditional 'dramatic theatre' which Brecht repudiated. More importantly, John Gwilym Jones, unlike Brecht, expected his audiences *to identify themselves emotionally with Morgan Llwyd.* The title itself – it is the title of one of Llwyd's own poems, written in 1650 recalling his turbulent life – suggests that Llwyd's story should be regarded, to quote the playwright himself, as *the story of any Welshman or Englishman or Frenchman whoever he might be.*

In 1971 a collection of short plays which John Gwilym Jones had written between 1961 and 1968 was published under the unassuming title PEDAIR DRAMA (*Four Plays*). The titles of these plays are: HYNT PEREDUR (*Peredur's Progress*); PRY FFENAST (*A Window Fly*); YR OEDFA (*The Service*); A BARCUD YN FARCUD FYTH (*And a Kite is a Kite for ever*).

The central theme of HYNT PEREDUR, a radio play written in 1962, echoes HANES RHYW GYMRO in that it deals with an individual having to come to terms

74

with disillusionment, in this particular case, political disillusionment. However, there is also a complementary and more intimate theme: sexual inhibition.

Peredur, a schoolboy who is profoundly conscious of the significance of his name – it was Peredur (Percival) in Arthurian legend who was granted sight of the Holy Grail – presumes that he too is destined for a unique mission in life. But this Peredur has misgivings about his quest and imagines himself in a court-room being cross-examined by a judge who warns of the perils that could befall him:

A JUDGE'S VOICE: . . . But there it is, a man who calls himself Peredur is different from everybody else.
PEREDUR: It's a name that has tradition.
A JUDGE'S VOICE: That's exactly what I'm saying. And there's danger in being too conscious of the past and tradition.

Peredur decides to campaign for Plaid Cymru in a by-election. An independent Wales will be the 'Grail' which he pursues. But despite his impassioned and vociferous campaigning his party comes bottom of the poll. Peredur is resentful and devastated. Perhaps, after all, he is no different from ordinary mortals:

A JUDGE'S VOICE: Go home, John Jones, my darling, as fast as you can . . . Plant your head on your mummy's bosom, that's the only safe place . . .

An admirer of his, Jane Rhiannon, whose name is a fitting combination of the ordinary and the heroic, helps Peredur to come to terms with his dis-illusionment, not so much by encouraging him to forsake politics but by instilling in him a *sense of proportion*:

JANE: . . . but we must keep trying.
PEREDUR: If winning an election for the party is the important thing to you. Remember there are also other important things.

It is at this point in the play that the other theme is introduced. Having come to terms with his 'political' idealism, Peredur now has to come to terms with his sexless 'romantic' idealism. Unconsciously, he has fallen in love with 'Rhiannon' rather than with 'Jane':

JANE: . . . I have a middle name.
PEREDUR: I know what it is, too.
JANE: What?
PEREDUR: Rhiannon
JANE: Because I'm such a loud-mouth?
PEREDUR: Because I prefer Rhiannon to all the women in the Mabinogi.

He is forced to confront life's sexuality when William Hughes, his widowed mother's lover – Peredur is as yet unaware of this relationship – confesses that he too is in love. Peredur is overwhelmed by revulsion:

PEREDUR: (seriously) Do you . . .?
W. HUGHES: Do I what?
PEREDUR: You know . . . play around with her . . . kiss?
W. HUGHES: If I said I did, would there be anything wrong with that?
PEREDUR: (obviously believing otherwise) No, there wouldn't.

His revulsion is exacerbated when at last he learns from his mother that she and William Hughes are to

76

marry. The play ends with a powerful symbolic scene in which his confused conscience and Jane's voice vie for his allegiance. The former urges him to abandon everything:

A JUDGE'S VOICE: . . . Welcome, John Jones, to the joy of oblivion . . .

But the latter reproaches him for his immaturity. Peredur has to confront life's sexuality:

JANE'S VOICE: What do you think your mother is? A lump of ice which is supposed to melt for nobody but you? What do you expect me to be at forty? A frigid nun?

And it is Jane who is the victor. Peredur rejoins his life-journey it is hoped as a more mature individual.

PEREDUR: What shall I say to mother?
JANE'S VOICE: Not a word. There's no need to say anything. Open the door, that's all . . . that will be enough. Open it, Peredur . . .
        PEREDUR opens the door.

This play is arguably the most optimistic in this collection in that the principal character is offered hope of a new and meaningful existence. At the end, Peredur's idealism is intact, if modified, and his sexual inhibition has relaxed a little. It is unfortunate that the complex psychological relationship between mother and son which occasions Peredur's sexual *angst*, has not been sufficiently explored. As a result, it could be argued that the play's two themes have not been successfully consolidated. Every inter-pretation, however ingenious, appears after close scrutiny to be frustratingly inadequate. Reluctantly one has to conclude that the playwright was perhaps too ambitious in attempting to grapple with two such profound themes within the confines of a short play.

PRY FFENAST was written for the radio in 1961, and concerns a widow's futile attempt to escape from her wretched past. Dora, whose husband has recently committed suicide in the wake of an affair, is offered hope of a new life in America when an old college boyfriend, Eifion, proposes to her. The only stumbling-block is her son Huw, for whom she has bought a farm from the proceeds of her husband's estate. After an emotional and candid exchange between Huw and Dora about his father's infidelity, Huw reconciles himself to Dora's decision to marry and emigrate. Indeed, it appears that he, too, is about to marry. But Dora's hopes are frustrated when she discovers that Huw, unwittingly, has fallen in love with her husband's former lover, Madge. She is determined that Huw, who has inherited his father's personality traits, should not also suffer the same fate.

The last scene, in which Dora confronts Madge, is the most poignant. It has become evident from earlier scenes that Madge is not an opportunistic slut but a sophisticated and sensitive woman who, unlike the anguished Dora, has come to terms with life's inevitable complexities:

MADGE: (tenderly, self-controlled) Listen, Mrs Richards. Not that I'm about to try to justify myself in any way, I know as well as anybody that there is no justification for what happened. The whole affair was sordid and sad. I shall never never forget it . . . I shall never never get rid of the shame . . . but there's no sense in allowing one unlucky incident . . .
DORA: Unlucky?

MADGE: Yes, Mrs Richards, unlucky. There's no sense in allowing that one incident to prevent me from . . . well, being as happy as I can be from now on.

For a moment, it appears that Dora, rather reluctantly, will have to accept the inevitable and that Huw will never be told the truth. But when Madge tells her that she and Huw have already married, Dora is inconsolable. The play ends on a note of sheer despair; even the self-assured Eifion finds himself having to share Dora's emotional entrapment. Perhaps with Eifion's help and understanding she will eventually overcome her bitterness but this is by no means certain:

EIFION: . . . (Dora's crying from now on gradually quietens down so that there will be only silence at the end.) Don't you worry. Everything will be all right. Only you and I. Together, there will be nothing to fear. Nothing at all, Dora . . . my love . . . my dear love . . .

As John Rowlands has suggested, we are compelled to judge Dora for her reluctance to consign the past, despite its traumas, to oblivion. Her contempt for Madge is not motivated by moral imperatives – in fact she is an atheist – but by irrational possessiveness. Peredur's problem was his inherent fear of embracing human emotions; Dora's problem is that she allows them free rein and as a consequence they destroy her life.

What makes PRY FFENAST stand out as one of John Gwilym Jones's most accomplished plays is the fact that his characters are not prone to tedious and unnecessary self-analysis. Instead he allows the dramatic action and the ironic exchanges to convey the central theme.

There are striking similarities between YR OEDFA, written for radio in 1968, and 'Y Briodas', one of the short stories in Y GOEDEN EIRIN. In both, our attention is focused upon an individual's private yearnings during a religious service. Like Jimmy Porter in John Osborne's LOOK BACK IN ANGER (which John Gwilym Jones translated and directed in 1965 under the title CILWG YN ÔL) Ifor, a teacher of religious studies, is an arrogant and resentful young man who delights in needling his wife Dilys. What provokes his fury on this particular occasion is having to attend chapel to listen to Dilys's father preaching. But, unlike the impassive Alison in Osborne's play, Dilys does retaliate. Indeed, they are a couple who, despite their constant bickering, *understand each other well* according to the stage directions.

During the service we cut from the sermon to Ifor's imaginings in which he gives free rein to his frustrations. In his imagination, he is about to be interviewed for a headmaster's post and he delights in demeaning a pompous local alderman:

ALDERMAN: I have heard that you're applying for the post of Headmaster at Tanydref.
IFOR: Oh, and you've heard that?
ALDERMAN: And I was wondering whether you'd be willing to honour me . . .
IFOR: Yes?
ALDERMAN: Give me permission to vote for you. You'd allow me to vote for you.

After he has been prompted by parts of the sermon to compose absurd limericks, there follows a symbolic scene in which he visualizes himself being part of a trapeze double-act with his father-in-law, the two of them *bound together in sheer hate*. It appears that his father-in-law is the embodiment of all that Ifor loathes: respectability.

But Ifor is unexpectedly reminded of the dangers of rejecting respectability. During one of the imaginary trapeze displays his father-in-law deliberately drops him. The symbolic significance of this act is terrifyingly apparent to Ifor: respectability has power over life and death. One has to conform or face the consequences. It is at this point that Ifor becomes acutely aware of his inherent frailty and, as Dilys has predicted earlier, of the *greatness of his fall* were it ever to happen:

DILYS: (quietly) What's the matter with you?
IFOR: (confused) You're all sweat . . .

Another blow is dealt to his self-esteem when he imagines his pupils detecting his lack of religious faith. Even his own individualistic religious vision which he has attempted to capture in a poem is met with derision. Aware of his personal shortcomings, he has no choice but to turn to Dilys:

IFOR: Hold my hand.
DILYS: Don't be silly.
IFOR: Dil, hold my hand . . .
DILYS: People will see.
IFOR: Let them . . . if you could only hold . . . only hold . . .
Thanks . . . Thank you . . .

YR OEDFA is a dextrously written piece which exploits the medium of radio to the full. Because Ifor is only able to realize his yearnings in his imagination no harm befalls anyone; even his humiliation is imaginary.

The main character in A BARCUD YN FARCUD FYTH decides to realize his yearnings in real life, with embarrassing and humiliating consequences. This play, which was written for television in 1966, takes its title from a poem by the sixteenth-century poet Siôn Tudur.

It begins with Ted, a wimpish teacher of Welsh, being patronized and demeaned by his obnoxious headmaster, and consequently deciding to change his image and personality. After buying trendy new shoes he goes home to his wife, Lil, and lies to her about his exchange with his headmaster:

LIL: *And what did you say?*
TED: *Do I have to say it more than once?*
LIL: *Do what you want, but it would be easier for me to understand, wouldn't it?*
TED: *Very well. 'Go to hell', that's what I said.*

Ted *for the first time in [his] life has dared to do something real, something exciting.* Shocked and disgusted by her *reborn* husband and his newly discovered *glorious freedom,* she orders him out of the house.

After flirting pathetically with Lal, a young girl, and evading his minister, he audaciously enters a pub to celebrate his rebirth. Unfortunately Mark, a former pupil of his, is already there celebrating his degree result. Assisted by Jac, an unusually learned milkman, he deliberately sets about humiliating Ted by insinuating that Lil might be having an affair. At the end of the scene, unable to retaliate, and ridiculed by everyone present, Ted runs away.

When he arrives home he learns, much to his embarrassment, that Lil has been to see his headmaster. But, conscious of Ted's predicament, she is sympathetic and forgiving:

TED: (breaking his heart) *O Lil, please, please don't you laugh . . . don't you laugh . . .*
LIL: (holding him tenderly) *There . . . there . . . everything's all right . . .*

However hard we try, we cannot alter our personalities. Hope of a rebirth is no more than a cruel illusion.

Themes similar to those of his earlier plays are again explored in a trilogy of short stage plays published in 1976 under the title RHYFEDD Y'N GWNAED (*Wondrously Made*). In TRI CHYFAILL (*Three Friends*) we encounter three men, Dan, Twm and Em who have gone away together on a short break. However, because of the rain, they are forced to idle indoors at their hotel. It is then that intimate details about their personal lives are revealed. Twm, aggrieved by Em's remarks about his childless marriage, confesses to Dan that – unknown to Em – he is the father of Em's child. Ironically, Twm is not aware of the fact that Dan is having an affair with his own wife. It is only Em who knows about Dan's affair, and he is nauseated by this betrayal of friendship. However, it is assumed that neither Twm nor Em will be told the truth. Candour and a contented life make uneasy bedfellows.

What is significant is that neither Dan nor Twm are proud of their actions. It is the seemingly amoral Dan, in an ironic exchange with Twm, the cuckold, who is acutely aware of life's intrinsic paradoxes:

DAN: . . . sometimes laughter is akin to crying . . . Do you understand that?
TWM: . . . Yes in a way, I think I do.

The ironies implicit in the situation are, as one might expect, exploited to the full; unfortunately, at times they seem contrived and crude:

TWM: (a cold statement only) If I knew that someone was treating Ceinwen like I'm treating Sali, I'd kill him.

It could also be argued that Dan and Em's closing remarks are superfluous since their message is implied by the characters' actions:

EM: But between friends, we must shut up, mustn't we?
DAN: Yes Em . . . Between friends we must shut up, mustn't we?

In the second play, DWY YSTAFELL (Two Rooms), two students, Meic and Lis have arranged a date. Despite the fact that behind his locked door Meic delights in soft pornography, he wants to give the impression to his fellow-students that he is a sophisticated playboy. He ridicules his friend Huw's sexual innocence: The only arousal you dare to satisfy is when you're alone in your bed surrounded by your nude pictures . . .

Similarly, Lis, bored by the pretentiousness of college

life, wants to give the impression to her friend Nel that she is seeking a sexual adventure. She is not in any way perturbed by Nel's warnings about Meic:

NEL: *But the rumours there are about him.*
LIS: *Let's hope they're true.*

When the two of them actually meet in Lis's room, it is no surprise that Meic, when faced with reality, is not the playboy he likes to believe. Rather than 'undressing' and seducing Lis, he begins to deride Huw's dull conformity. In fact, Meic is symbolically exposing his own true self: *There's a part of him that makes me mad . . . that disgusts me . . . seeing a part of him for what he is . . .* And Lis has indeed realized this:

LIS: *And now, how about getting dressed.*
MEIC: (saying it, only) *Getting dressed.*
LIS: *You've exposed yourself for far too long, haven't you?*
MEIC: (understanding her remark) *I have, haven't I?*

It is only after Meic's intimate confession that the two are able to relate to each other physically. But the passion is short-lived; Meic's unexpected confession has rather dampened Lis's passion.

Nel returns, and out of sheer vanity Lis leads her to believe that they have indeed made love. When Lis talks about her experience Nel is unaware of the fact that she is talking figuratively:

LIS: *. . . Nudity is not a pretty sight.*
NEL: *Don't, Lis, don't . . .*
LIS: *Don't ever believe anyone who says that it is. Nudity is filthy . . . filthy . . . a sordid exposure of oneself . . .*

Whilst Lis has learnt that intimacy can be both meaningful and harrowing, it appears that Meic has learnt nothing from this experience. Rather than tearing up his pornography – though for a brief moment he appears to be about to do so – he puts it back into the drawer. Rather than face up to his cowardly self and, with Lis's help, enter into a candid, normal, perhaps often difficult, human relationship, the temptation to keep up appearances is overwhelming. Meic cannot change his nature: it is doubtful whether he will return to Lis's room.

The most regularly performed play in this trilogy is UN BRIODAS (*One Wedding*). Employing monologues, duettist dialogue and flashbacks, the play explores the reasons for the breakdown of Dic and Meg's marriage. Their wedding-day was extraordinarily joyous:

MEG: *A fine early spring morning.*
DIC: *The fields all the way to the chapel white with open daisies.*
MEG: *Each daisy flaunting its yellow centre in every field on the way to the chapel.*

The couple were the embodiment of youthful innocence:

DIC: *Faith.*
MEG: *Faith.*
DIC: *Hope.*
MEG: *Hope.*
DIC: *Love.*
MEG: *Love.*
DIC: *I was a virgin.*
MEG: *I was a virgin.*

But Dic, incensed by an uncle's seemingly innocent yet suggestive remarks about offspring, made during the reception, resolves not to touch Meg on their wedding-night despite the fact that he loves her dearly. Bitterly convinced that Dic has rejected her, Meg is overcome by a similar obstinacy: *I'll never forget this, I said to myself. Never, never, never . . . I'll show him! I too can be stubborn.*

This intransigence causes a total lack of communication between the couple. What little sex they experience is attended by feelings of revulsion:

MEG: *The whole thing is disgusting . . .*
DIC: *I feel . . .*
MEG: *Filthy . . .*
DIC: *. . . as if I'm . . .*
MEG: *A sin .*
DIC: *. . . raping her every time.*

Nevertheless they keep up appearances. At times Dic experiences *sudden unexpected moments of hope.* Seeing Meg wearing a new dress reminds him of happier days which he longs to recapture, such as the occasion when they first met at Llyn Dywarchen. But Meg is unresponsive:

DIC: *. . . Where would you like to go? Llyn Dywarchen?*
MEG: *No.*
DIC: *All right then, somewhere else. A dinner at Beddgelert. You in your new dress.*
MEG: *This isn't an evening dress.*

Eventually Dic meets another woman but confesses that she is no more than a re-embodiment of Meg as she used to be *a long long time ago.* But it is this affair that foreshadows their separation. At the end of the play they are two solitary and confused individuals tragically unwilling to convey their anguish to each other:

MEG: O Dic, what's going to happen to us?
DIC: Meg, Meg what's going to happen to us?

It is not only the couple's inherent stubbornness which needlessly wrecks their marriage. Dic is probably more at fault than Meg and his stubbornness is arguably an outward manifestation of a deeper problem. Like Peredur, Dic can respond only to romantic, sexless love. He cannot reconcile the Meg with whom he became infatuated on the shores of Llyn Dywarchen with the woman's body beside him in bed: Meg is *the holy thing* there beside him not *the one who will be the mother of his children*. Unfortunately, she too is obstinate and is unable to allay his fears. Peredur was more fortunate: Jane, a more generous individual, was able to do so and thus Peredur is saved from the potential destructiveness of his instincts.

The three plays were translated by the author and produced in New York in 1980 by the Manhattan Theater Club. Reviewing the production in the SOHO WEEKLY NEWS, Donald R. Wilson wrote:

Jones is a master of contrasting appearances with hidden realities and these superbly performed playlets reflect his control of both irony and craft. These are superior charming dramatic vignettes.

AC ETO NID MYFI (*And Yet Not I*), which was published in 1976, represented the culmination of fifty years of dramatic writing. It was to a large extent biographical, although he was anxious to emphasize that he had never *fathered an illegitimate child!* Its deterministic theme is implicit in most if not all of his previous works but in this play it is explored in depth.

The title comes from a poem by T. H. Parry-Williams whose bleak and ironic vision of life he had always found appealing. The poem is entitled 'Dryswch' (*Confusion*) and in it the poet perceives the paradoxes inherent in human identity. His own identity, the poet asserts, is made up of a multitude of differing and conflicting peculiarities which appear to him to have a bewildering existence of their own; yet he has to conclude that these peculiarities, alien though they appear to him, are what constitute his identity.

> *There are so many of us in my clay,*
> *A myriad in my being, each one his cry.*
> *Each one his virtue, each one his fault.*
> *Strangers are we all, – yet it is I.*
>
> *One's virtue differs little from one's fault*
> *And in the chaos how estranged the cry.*
> *There are so many of us in my clay*
> *And I am all of these, – and yet not I.*

(tr. Dewi Jones)

Huw, the main character, experiences similar feelings to those expressed by the poet. At the beginning of the play after his offer of marriage has been rejected by his pregnant girlfriend Alis, he ponders in a lengthy morose monologue the *despotic, indifferent, merciless powers* which have fashioned his personality. Environment is likened to a despot: *He sits on his throne and we inescapably are his subjects, having been tailored to his exact measurements; enslaved in his uniform.* But it is heredity which is the more ominous force: *Every little child [is] born pregnant [and] carries the illegitimate child of his past.* The play proceeds to delineate in poignant detail how these instrumental forces have fashioned Huw's personality and life.

The most significant influence upon him in his immediate environment is his own home. Even at an early age Huw is overwhelmed by fears and anxieties: *Going to bed was what worried me. In the bedroom alone, and fear staring at me in the candle-light. I had to make sure that Mother was in the house . . .* But his mother, whom he *thinks the world of*, is reluctant to allay these anxieties:

HUW: *Give me a kiss.*
MOTHER: *Don't be silly.*
HUW: *Please, Mother, give me a kiss.*
MOTHER: *No, I won't. You're far too big a lad for that now.*
HUW: (to the audience) *How old was I? Five? Six? Seven?*

His anxieties are exacerbated by his mother's uncompromising Calvinism and her deep-rooted suspicion of sexuality. One of the most powerful scenes in the play is the one in which Huw out of sheer mischievousness utters an obscene word in his mother's presence:

MOTHER: (having lost all control of herself) *What did you say? What did you say?*
HUW: (fearful, yet defiant) *That's what Sami calls it. That's what all the boys except me call it.* (His mother gives him a really sharp clout and the two weep.)

The pain inflicted by his mother's clout will haunt his relationship with Alis. After their first meeting Huw remarks:

HUW: *(to the audience) I've never been so recklessly happy, so insanely at peace with myself. And yet the pain of mother's clout is like a live coal on my cheek. (to Alis) Are you all right now?*
ALIS: *Yes.* (No kissing. Huw takes her handkerchief to wipe her tears.)

Before long Alis realizes that their relationship is unfulfilling: *Every time you . . . kiss me, a part of you is elsewhere.* Both become keenly aware of the paradoxes inherent in their respective natures. Huw is perplexed by Alis's inconsistency with regard to their sexual relationship:

HUW: *You believe in all these things and yet you're willing to . . .*
ALIS: *To what?*
HUW: *To do all these things that you and I do.*
ALIS: *What's difficult to understand in that?*
HUW: *Rather inconsistent aren't you?*

And she is equally perplexed by him:

ALIS: *More inconsistent than yourself?*
HUW: *Who do you mean?*
ALIS: *You believe nothing and yet you're ashamed to do them.*

Huw is destined to become an outsider tormented by life's inconsistencies and ultimately its absurdity.

Yet, as Elan Closs Stephens contends in Y CANOL LLONYDD (*The Still Centre*), this religious culture, despite the damage it has inflicted upon him, is a more potent force in Huw's life than his atheism. Having convinced himself at his father's funeral that religion is no more than *a futile rigmarole*, he then *has to sing* at the graveside.

When Huw first learns that Alis is pregnant, his instinctive reaction is to commit suicide. He is prevented from doing so by the voice of his landlady singing a hymn from his childhood, 'I know that my Redeemer liveth'. As Elan Closs Stephens points out it is *this memory of the religious past which enables Huw to return home*. He is saved from despair not only by his mother's readiness to forgive – and it is ironic that he seeks the forgiveness of the person who has wrecked his life – but also by his willingness to accept the contradictions and inconsistencies within himself. He is able to face the future *without being blinded*. Elan Closs Stephens maintains that *he has arrived at the still centre*. It is difficult to accept this assertion in the light of Huw's somewhat cheerless and unemotional concluding remark: *I am, despite everything, going to be allowed to live . . . live . . . live . . .*

When it was first performed, many were critical of the play's lack of theatricality because the main character is allowed to analyse his feelings in lengthy monologues. However, it could be argued that this criticism is short-sighted. What Huw cannot do is divulge his inner feelings to Alis. It is his inherent reticence which alienates him from her. Ironically he is only on intimate terms with the audience. Such irony is arguably more theatrically powerful than mere spectacle which, regrettably, some theatre practitioners appear to regard as the essence of drama.

Writing his last play YR ADDUNED (*The Vow*) was a particularly harrowing experience for John Gwilym Jones. The National Eisteddfod had been invited to Caernarfon in 1979 and the Drama Committee had commissioned him to write a new play. The chairman of this committee was his lifelong friend, William Vaughan Jones (Wil Fôn). Sadly, Vaughan Jones died shortly after John Gwilym Jones had accepted the commission. Overcome with grief, he found himself unable to write. Indeed the grief and frustration led to his experiencing a mild nervous breakdown. But rather than abandon the project and break a vow to an old friend he decided to write a play analysing his own creative impasse. It is the most personal of his works.

In Act One 'Ifan I' is in a similar situation to that of John Gwilym Jones. He has vowed to *a close . . . dear friend* that he would write a play but is unable to do so. He is visited by 'Ifan II' who appears to be his creative self. Ifan II orders him to begin searching for inspiration within himself, employing all his sensual faculties:

IFAN II: Listen . . . Stare . . . Taste . . . Smell . . . Feel . . . Think and think . . . Search and search . . . that's what you'll do.
IFAN I: But where?
IFAN II: Within yourself . . . in your knowledge of people . . . of life . . . in the life-giving pool of your unconscious . . . where my home is.

Prompted by Ifan II he recalls scenes from his past life which could be potentially inspiring. With one particular exception these scenes either underline Ifan I's inability to accept death or, more poignantly, his inability to accept life's sexuality.

It is Elis Huws, an old widower dying of cancer, who makes Ifan I aware of life's inherent horrors:

ELIS HUWS: Your turn will come.
IFAN I: (saying it only) My turn.
ELIS HUWS: Your sorrow . . . your despair . . . your loneliness.
IFAN I: My tears?
ELIS HUWS: Yes, your tears also.

Visiting Meri and Ianto was a means of escaping from this knowledge. In their company, Ifan I was only conscious of life's joys. Meri, despite being in her own words *an ugly woman*, is still in Ianto's eyes *as beautiful as ever*. When Ianto gives him some apples, Ifan I asks for *one more apple* which, to his naïve and immature mind, will always symbolize life's potential bliss. In fact, as Elan Closs Stephens has pointed out, it symbolizes the sexuality with which he will eventually have to come to terms.

At the time he could not come to terms with Ianto and Meri's mortality either. Death was something to be mocked. During this scene Ifan I humorously mentions a *plank* to which dead bodies were tied for burial. It, like the *apple*, has a symbolic significance – amidst the apparent bliss, death lurks:

IFAN II: This is the first time I've ever heard about the plank.
IFAN I: It comes to everybody and everything.

As far as the *play* is concerned it appears that this recollection has potential. More potential perhaps than Ifan I's recollection of a confrontation between himself and his headmaster. Ifan I has strong nationalist convictions and when accused by his headmaster of brainwashing his pupils he responds angrily:

IFAN I: . . . *How can I explain Robert Williams Parry's best poems without telling them that they flowed from within him when he became enraged by the inhuman treatment that Saunders Lewis experienced for burning the Bombing School at Penyberth . . .*

But political convictions do not necessarily produce great art. Great art stems from self-knowledge, an agonizing awareness of one's failings.

In this respect, recollections of his visit to Bet after her husband's sudden death could prove fruitful. Ifan I is told bluntly by Bet that he had nothing to offer her except platitudes:

IFAN I: (getting up, putting his hand on Bet's shoulder) *That's it Bet . . . that's it . . . tears help.*
BET: *Everybody says that too . . .*

It was in his relationship with Cit that Ifan I had to confront his failings. He had hoped that their relationship would be similar to that of Meri and Ianto. But Ifan I is no Ianto: Ianto has accepted life's sexuality and has fathered a daughter, Lisi, who significantly *loves being given her father's apples*. But Ifan I cannot *take a bite out of the apple*, and as a consequence Cit realizes that their relationship is doomed:

IFAN I: *What could happen?*
CIT: *Things.*
IFAN I: *Things?*
CIT: *All kind of things.*

We are not explicitly told what these *things* which would eventually have wrecked their lives are. One can assume that they are sexual in nature and that the *play* if it were ever written, would be about this doomed relationship.

Because of the complex interplay between Ifan I and Ifan II and the grotesque imagery employed in the closing scenes, which according to Elan Closs Stephens has sexual connotations, this is John Gwilym Jones's most enigmatic play. In trying to impose his own logic upon Ifan I's recollections the critic finds himself assuming the role of the dramatist and forgetting that perhaps the *play* had actually been written in the form of AC ETO NID MYFI three years earlier!

John Gwilym Jones's last work, published in 1979, was the novel TRI DIWRNOD AC ANGLADD (*Three Days and a Funeral*). It can be summarized as follows:

Elwyn Price, a television newsreader, receives a letter from his father Edward requesting him to return to his home, Plas-y-Ddôl, which he has not visited for five years. His decision to keep away from the family home was a conscious one; he had only traumatic memories of the place. During his childhood, his mother Nina, had shown little affection towards him. Because she was pregnant with Elwyn at the time of her marriage she held him responsible for the indignity she had to endure.

When Elwyn arrives at the house all appears changed and decaying. His parents, despite living in the same house, live separate lives. The father, Edward, once a *a tall graceful man* is now *a pitiful bundle* who derives comfort from his books, his alcohol and the company of Lisi, the elderly nanny with whom he shares his bed. As a consequence Lisi in not allowed to care for Elwyn's mother Nina, who is terminally ill with cancer. Although visited by Gwen, Elwyn's sister, and her husband Ted, Nina is cared for by Rob, Edward's simple-minded son from his first marriage.

The other characters in the novel are the local GP, Dr Rita Gibbs and her daughter Eurgain, a precocious intelligent schoolgirl and a militant member of the Welsh Language Society.

It becomes apparent to Elwyn that it was not Edward who had written the letter calling him home. It was written by Rob at Nina's prompting. Conscious of her impending death, Nina has called Elwyn home to arrange her divorce. Nina wants *to die free*. Elwyn and Gwen, hoping that their mother would die before a divorce came through, agree to comply with her request.

Nina dies and the inevitable embarrassment which would have accompanied a divorce appears to have been avoided. But it was not her illness which killed Nina: she was poisoned by Rob because he did not want his father to be hurt. Dr Gibbs is anxious to inform the coroner, but after a rather bizarre scene in which Elwyn makes love to her, she decides not to do so. In accordance with her wishes Nina's body is cremated and Elwyn departs from Plas-y-Ddôl.

This novel is like the play AC ETO NID MYFI in that it is about an individual being forced to confront his past which, in this particular case, he has made a conscious effort to reject. Elwyn has tried to create a new identity for himself by becoming a newsreader, whose function is to report dispassionately and objectively upon events. His obsession with fashionable clothes symbolizes his attempt to create this new persona for himself. But it is a job that ill suits his real personality because throughout the novel he divulges in minute detail his most intimate emotions. For a man who has decided to forget his past he has particularly vivid memories of his home and its inhabitants.

The damage inflicted upon Elwyn is symbolized by the *dent* on the bonnet of his car which Rob makes during one of his inexplicable fits of rage as Elwyn first approaches the house. Rob's attempts throughout the novel to repair this *dent* symbolically parallel Elwyn's attempt to repair his own *dented* personality. This he does by coming to accept not only life's paradoxes but also the conflicting emotions within himself. When his father informs him of his relationship with Lisi he is overwhelmed by disgust, yet he is forced to conclude that their relationship is inevitable, even *normal*. Although angered by his mother's deviousness, her condition means that he cannot but forgive her:

Against my will and nearly crying I faced up to the fairness of her wish . . . I found myself warm with sympathy and mercy in thinking about her frail existence in her barren land, and her courage – what other word was there? – in facing her end so boldly.

The sub-plot involving Dr Gibbs and Eurgain is ingeniously woven into the main plot. Elwyn becomes infatuated with both mother and daughter. However it appears that Eurgain, much to Elwyn's chagrin and disgust, is having a covert affair with Ted, Gwen's husband. Paradoxically, knowledge of this affair not only enables Elwyn to see his aloof brother-in-law in a new and sympathetic light, but also enables him to catch a glimpse of Gwen's inherent compassion, a quality which he himself so lacks. When for purely selfish motives he seduces Dr Gibbs, he discovers that she too is using him. Elwyn is no more than a sexual substitute for her estranged husband.

Elwyn departs from Plas-y-Ddôl having experienced a kind of personal purgatory. The hurt, like the *dent* on the car bonnet, is still there but he will *force [himself] to become accustomed to [it]*. Elwyn has, to quote a phrase echoed throughout the novel, *grown up*.

~

To appreciate John Gwilym Jones's contribution to Welsh drama, we need to examine briefly the growth of modern Welsh theatre.

The rise of Nonconformity in the eighteenth and nineteenth centuries in Wales, and the conscious attempt to promote a culture based upon religious precepts resulted in a decline in secular dramatic activity. The *anterliwt* (interlude), a traditional form of dramatic entertainment, was ostracized because of the immorality and licentiousness which allegedly accompanied its performances. Despite deliberate attempts by Twm o'r Nant, the best-known writer of interludes, to reinforce the interlude's moral content, the tradition came to an end after his death in 1810. As a result, the interlude audiences often turned to the English touring companies for dramatic entertainment.

The revival, when it came, was gradual but sustained. Towards the middle of the nineteenth century attempts were made to employ drama for purely moral purposes. In periodicals such as Y CRONICL BACH short *ymddiddanion* (conversations) were published which dramatized moral issues and Biblical narratives. These attempts at dramatic writing were overtly didactic and ponderous in style.

However, in the second half of the nineteenth century, as a reaction against what the Welsh establishment considered to be a gross misrepresentation of the state of Welsh education in the infamous government-commissioned report of 1847 which came to be known as *Brad y Llyfrau Gleision* (The Treason of the Blue Books), there was a deliberate attempt to cultivate dramatic taste. The National Eisteddfod began to offer prizes for translations from Shakespeare, and in 1884 it introduced competitions for the writing of original plays. The most celebrated playwright of this period was Beriah Gwynfe Evans who was the editor of CYFAILL YR AELWYD (*The Hearthside Companion*) from 1881 until 1894. Inspired by the nationalist fervour of late nineteenth-century Welsh Liberalism, he composed a number of what he considered to be historical plays in Shakespearean style, delineating the patriotic exploits of illustrious Welsh heroes such as Owain Glyndŵr and Llywelyn the last native Prince of Wales.

But true resurgence came when the works of Daniel Owen, the late nineteenth-century Welsh novelist, began to be adapted for the stage. The first of his novels to receive this treatment was RHYS LEWIS in 1886. According to Dafydd Glyn Jones, whose seminal work on this period is invaluable to historians of modern Welsh drama, the adaptations focused on two crucial incidents in the novel. Rhys, the minister, has a brother Bob, who is wrongly imprisoned. In the only extant adaptation, made by J. M. Edwards in 1909, this incident is central to the dramatic plot. It is as if the adaptor deliberately wanted to focus the audience's attention, to quote Dafydd Glyn Jones, upon *a talented, intelligent, honest young man's battle . . . either for social justice or for the truth in a narrow pharisaical society which fears the truth.*

This *talented, intelligent, honest young man* would eventually become the principal hero of early twentieth-century plays by playwrights such as R. G. Berry, D. J. Davies, D. T. Davies, J. O. Francis (in translation) and W. J. Gruffydd. In their plays the hero more often than not directly challenges not only the values of the religious establishment but those of their parents.

Dafydd Glyn Jones also asserts that the adaptations introduced an additional element. Employing material from another of Daniel Owen's novels, ENOC HUWS, the witty lovable rogue Wil Bryan is brought back at the end of the play and becomes a member of the *seiat*, an institution within Calvinistic Methodist chapels for the spiritually-elect. In the original novel, conscious of his father's financial troubles, Wil Bryan flees from the town and does not return until his bankrupt father has died. In the original novel Wil is a calculating coward. In the adaptation he returns as the prosperous hero, as the reformed prodigal son, and according to Dafydd Glyn Jones, as *the restorer of the old life and saviour of the home.*

In the plays of the early twentieth century, the hero on his return home is seen as a *restorer* and *saviour* of that home. In W. J. Gruffydd's BEDDAU'R PROFFWYDI (*The Graves of the Prophets*) the hero Emrys declares:

> *EMRYS: . . . I've come to start again . . . on my great work.*
> *HUW BENNETT: What's that, my boy?*
> *EMRYS: To take hold of the plough with both hands and to teach Llanfesach to turn a straighter furrow . . . that's all.*

Dafydd Glyn Jones emphasized these characteristics of early twentieth-century plays in order to illustrate the extent to which the playwright Saunders Lewis manipulated them in his work. It is equally important to understand John Gwilym Jones's position in relation to this tradition.

His main characters, despite having been born into a similar society, are in sharp contrast to the heroes of these early plays in that they rarely challenge directly the religious establishment or their parents. Some are prompted to do so but with tragic consequences. Ifan's idealism in DIOFAL YW DIM leads to despair and nihilism, and when Gwyn out of sheer cussedness challenges his father in Y TAD A'R MAB it results in a murder. The majority of his protagonists are content just to be able to come to grips with life in all its complexities. They return home not as *restorers* or *saviours* but as disenchanted, broken souls in need of succour from either a mother or a wife.

The difference between the earlier playwrights and John Gwilym Jones lies in their opposing visions of life. Implicit in the works of R. G. Berry, D. J. Davies, D. T. Davies, J. O. Francis and W. J. Gruffydd is the belief that life, despite its injustices, is fundamentally meaningful if only individuals would act in a different way. John Gwilym Jones's vision of life is more pessimistic in that he embraces a deterministic view. He is first and foremost a 'naturalistic' playwright in the nineteenth-century European mould. 'Naturalistic' in this context is used in its original, historical, literary sense, to express the belief that human identity is the product of heredity and environment.

If this is so, then an individual's idealism, or indeed lack of idealism, is not prompted by a conscious commitment to objective principles but rather by a complex interplay of hereditary, psychological and cultural forces which act within and upon the individual. As a result the concept of good and evil becomes meaningless because no individual is responsible for his or her actions. Gwladys in LLE MYNNO'R GWYNT is forgiven by Alis, despite her anger, for helping Dewi to commit suicide; Robin in GŴR LLONYDD forgives Megan and tries to forget the past; by the end of Y TAD A'R MAB, Richard Owen, despite his perverse ambitions for his son Gwyn, commands our sympathy. Moral judgement is replaced by what is at the heart of all of John Gwilym Jones's work: compassion.

Bibliography

JOHN GWILYM JONES

Plays

Y BRODYR, Lerpwl, n.d.

DIOFAL YW DIM, Caerdydd, 1942.

DWY DDRAMA: LLE MYNNO'R GWYNT a GŴR LLONYDD, Dinbych, Gwasg Gee, 1958.

Y TAD A'R MAB, Aberystwyth, Gwasg y Glêr, 1963; Llandysul, Gwasg Gomer, 1970.

HANES RHYW GYMRO, Bangor, Cymdeithas y Cymric a Chymdeithas y Ddrama Gymraeg, Coleg Prifysgol Gogledd Cymru, 1964.

PEDAIR DRAMA (PRY FFENAST, HYNT PEREDUR, YR OEDFA, A BARCUD YN FARCUD FYTH), Dinbych, Gwasg Gee, 1971.

RHYFEDD Y'N GWNAED (TRI CHYFAILL, DWY YSTAFELL, UN BRIODAS), Dinbych, Gwasg Gee, 1976.

AC ETO NID MYFI, Dinbych, Gwasg Gee, 1976.

YR ADDUNED, Llandysul, Gwasg Gomer, 1979.

Television Adaptations

ENOC HUWS (Daniel Owen), BBC Wales, 1974.

GWEN TOMOS (Daniel Owen), BBC Wales, 1981.

Novels

Y DEWIS, Dinbych, Gwasg Gee, 1942.

A first chapter of an unpublished novel in YR ARLOESWR, 1 (Summer 1957) 14–24.

TRI DIWRNOD AC ANGLADD, Llandysul, Gwasg Gomer, 1979.

Short Stories

'Nychdod', Y FORD GRON, 1 (June 1931) 12–13.

Y GOEDEN EIRIN, Dinbych, Gwasg Gee, 1946.

'Dyletswydd', in STORÏAU'R DEFFRO, ed. Islwyn Ffowc Elis, Caerdydd, Plaid Cymru, 1959, 51–8.

Translations of Plays into Welsh

Published

YMWELIAD YR HEN FONEDDIGES (Friedrich Dürrenmatt; with G. L. Jones), Caerdydd, Gwasg Prifysgol Cymru, 1976.

Unpublished

CILWG YN ÔL (LOOK BACK IN ANGER, John Osborne).
Y CROCHAN (THE CRUCIBLE, Arthur Miller).
PWY SY'N IAWN? (THE COLLECTION, Harold Pinter).
YR ADUNIAD (THE FAMILY REUNION, T. S. Eliot).
FERSIWN BROWNING (THE BROWNING VERSION, Terence Rattigan).
NOSON ALLAN (NIGHT OUT, Harold Pinter).
GWAS A MEISTR (THE ADMIRABLE CRICHTON, J. M. Barrie).
CARTREF (HOME, David Storey).
TROI A THROSI (ROUND AND ROUND THE GARDEN, Alan Ayckbourn).
YR YSBÏWR (I SPY, John Mortimer).
YR YSTAFELL (THE ROOM, Harold Pinter).
BYDD WRTH EIN BWRDD (TABLE MANNERS, Alan Ayckbourn).
POPETH YN YR ARDD (EVERYTHING IN THE GARDEN, Edward Albee's adaptation of a play by Giles Cooper).

Autobiography

CAPEL AC YSGOL, (Annual Lecture of the Pen-y-groes Library), Caernarfon, Llyfrgell Sir Gaernarfon, 1970.

'Y Seiat oedd y Bwgan', Y GWRANDAWR: BARN, 101, (March 1971).

AR DRAWS AC AR HYD (Cyfres y Cewri), Caernarfon, Gwasg Gwynedd, 1986.

Biography

BRO A BYWYD – JOHN GWILYM JONES, ed. Manon Wyn Siôn, Llandybïe, Cyhoeddiadau Barddas, 1993.

Literary Criticism

WILLIAM WILLIAMS PANTYCELYN, Caerdydd, Gwasg Prifysgol Cymru, 1969 (Bilingual).

GORONWY OWEN'S VIRGINIAN ADVENTURE, Virginia, The Botetourt Bibliographical Society, College of William and Mary, 1969.

DANIEL OWEN, Dinbych, Gwasg Gee, 1979.

NOFELYDD YR WYDDGRUG (Daniel Owen Memorial Lecture), Yr Wyddgrug (Mold), Pwyllgor Ystafell Goffa Daniel Owen, 1976.

SWYDDOGAETH BEIRNIADAETH AC YSGRIFAU ERAILL, Dinbych, Gwasg Gee, 1977.

CREFFT Y LLENOR, Dinbych, Gwasg Gee, 1977.

YR ARWR YN Y THEATR (Astudiaethau Theatr Cymru 3), Bangor, Cymdeithas Theatr Cymru, 1981.

CRITICAL STUDIES

English

Rowlands, John, 'The Humane Existentialist – playwright John Gwilym Jones' in WELSH BOOKS AND WRITERS (Autumn 1980) 6–7.

Welsh

Jones, R. M., 'Easily Freudened', 'Tri Beirniad Seciwlar' and 'Hanes Rhyw Ddramodydd' in LLENYDDIAETH GYMRAEG 1936–1972, Llandybïe, Christopher Davies, 1975.

Rowlands, John, JOHN GWILYM JONES (Llên y Llenor), Caernarfon, Gwasg Pantycelyn, 1988.

Rowlands, John, 'Agweddau ar waith John Gwilym Jones', in YSGRIFAU BEIRNIADOL III, Dinbych, Gwasg Gee, 1967.

Rowlands, John, 'John Gwilym Jones', DYRNAID O AWDURON CYFOES, ed. D. Ben Rees, Pontypridd a Lerpwl, Cyhoeddiadau Modern Cymreig, 1975.

Rowlands, John, 'John Rowlands yn holi John Gwilym Jones', LLAIS LLYFRAU, (Spring 1980) 5–8.

Stephens, Elan Closs, Y CANOL LLONYDD (Astudiaethau Theatr Cymru 5), Cricieth, Cymdeithas Theatr Cymru, 1988.

Thomas, Gwyn (ed.), JOHN GWILYM JONES: CYFROL DEYRNGED, Llandybïe, Christopher Davies, 1974.

Thomas, Gwyn, 'Holi John Gwilym Jones', MABON, I, 3 (Summer 1970) 12–18.

Tomos, Gwennan, ASTUDIAETH O DDRAMÂU JOHN GWILYM JONES, unpublished MA thesis, Bangor, 1979.

Williams, J. Ellis, TRI DRAMAYDD CYFOES, Dinbych, Gwasg Gee, 1961.

GENERAL BACKGROUND

Jones, Dafydd Glyn, 'Y Ddrama Ryddiaith' in Y TRADDODIAD RHYDDIAITH YN YR UGEINFED GANRIF, ed. Geraint Bowen, Llandysul, Gwasg Gomer, 1976.

Jones, Dafydd Glyn, 'Saunders Lewis a thraddodiad y ddrama Gymraeg', LLWYFAN, 9 (Winter 1973) 1–12. (This pioneering study is also relevant to any study of John Gwilym Jones's contribution to modern Welsh theatre.)

Lewis, Saunders, CREFFT Y STORI FER, Llandysul, Y Clwb Llyfrau Cymraeg, 1949.

Acknowledgements

I should like to thank the following: my colleagues, Mr Dafydd Glyn Jones, Dr Bruce Griffiths, Mrs Branwen Jarvis and Mrs Glenda Carr, for their help in translating extracts from John Gwilym Jones's works; Mr Ned Thomas and Ruth Dennis-Jones of the University of Wales Press, for their valuable advice and support; Mr Dewi Jones for permission to use his translation of 'Dryswch'; and Mr Emyr Humphreys for permission to use extracts from his unpublished translation of Y TAD A'R MAB.

Author's Note

As no English translations of John Gwilym Jones's works have yet been published, I decided that it would be useful for those who are unable to read the original Welsh to have outlines of his main works. In so doing I am perhaps guilty in places of what the critic Cleanth Brooks called 'the heresy of paraphrase' and readers of Welsh may at times find this tedious. For this I apologize.

The Author

William R. Lewis was born in Llangristiolus, Ynys Môn, in 1948 and was raised there and in Llangefni. He attended Llangefni Secondary School before proceeding to the University College of North Wales, Bangor where he studied under John Gwilym Jones. After teaching at Ysgol Glan Clwyd, Llanelwy and at Ysgol Syr Thomas Jones, Amlwch, he returned to Bangor to lecture in the Drama Department at his old college. He is now lecturer in drama in the Department of Welsh at the University College of North Wales. As well as being a playwright and script-writer, he is an experienced theatre director and a member of Theatr Gwynedd's Artistic Panel.

Designed by Jeff Clements
Typesetting at the University of Wales Press
in 11pt Palatino and printed in Great Britain by
Qualitex Printing Limited, Cardiff, 1994.

British Library Cataloguing in Publication Data.

A catalogue record for this book is available from the British Library.

ISBN 0–7083–1251–9

The Publishers wish to acknowledge the financial assistance of the Welsh Arts Council towards the cost of producing this volume.